Bush Theatre

CW01467462

WOLVES ON ROAD

Beru Tessema

Wolves on Road premiered at the Bush Theatre,
London, on 9 November 2024.

WOLVES ON ROAD
by Beru Tessema

Cast

Fevan	Alma Eno
Abdul	Hassan Najib
Markos	Ery Nzaramba
Manny	Kieran Taylor-Ford
Devlin	Jamael Westman
	(9–23 November)
	Tom Moutchi (9–21 December)

Creative Team

Director	Daniel Bailey
Set & Costume Designer	Amelia Jane Hankin
Lighting Designer	Ali Hunter
Sound Designer & Composer	Duramaney Kamara
Video Designer	Gino Ricardo Green
Movement Director	Gabrielle Nimo
Assistant Director	Tatenda Shamiso
Fight Director	Kev McCurdy
Intimacy Director	Ingrid Mackinnon
Casting Director	Polly Jerrold
Casting Associate	Howard Hutt
Voice Coach	Gurkiran Kaur
Costume Supervisor	Georgia Wilmot
Make-up Supervisor	Sophia Khan
Production Manager	Lisa Hood
Company Stage Manager	Tayla Hunter
Assistant Stage Manager	Dynzell Muguti
Video Engineer	Ieuan Watkins-Hyde
Additional Production Carpentry	Chris Ashenden

This production is generously supported by Charles Holloway OBE.

For the Bush

Lead Producer	Oscar Owen
Dramaturg	Titilola Dawudu
Resident Director	Katie Greenall
Marketing Campaign Manager	Laela Henly-Rowe
Technical Manager	Jamie Haigh
Schools Project Lead & Community Producer	Holly Smith

For Tamasha

Producer	Bella Rodrigues
Assistant Director Recruitment & General Manager	Harris Albar
Marketing Manager	Rema Chandran

CAST

Alma Eno | Fevan

Alma trained at Mountview Academy of Theatre Arts.

Her theatre credits include: *Black Women Dating White Men* (Drayton Arms); *Take the Train* (Myriad Immersive/Pathway); *The Glass Will Shatter* (Omnibus); *Small Island* (National Theatre); *Champ* (Tobacco Factory); *Jessica* (Sheer Height Theatre Company); and *Marvel* (Project Arts Centre, Dublin).

Her television and film credits include: *Rose*; *Collision*; *Boogie Woogie*; *The Hound's Curse*; *Control Room*; *Road to Recovery*; *Intimacy RCA;* and the World Shakespeare Festival.

Hassan Najib | Abdul

Hassan is currently filming the new *Blade Runner 2009* series for Amazon and will next be seen as a leading role in Somali filmmaker K'naan's first feature film *Mother, Mother* premiering at the Toronto International Film Festival. Hassan was recently seen in *Dune: Part Two* and as the lead in the new feature film *Diamond Sky*. He has a regular role in international Sky drama *Unwanted*.

Ery Nzaramba | Markos

His theatre credits include: *Tempest Project, Why?, The Prisoner, Battlefield, The Suit* (world tours, dir. by Peter Brook); *Our Lady of Kibeho* (nominated for the Olivier Award for Outstanding Achievement in an Affiliate Theatre in 2020; Stratford East/Royal & Derngate); *Othellomacbeth* (Lyric Hammersmith/Home); *Split/Mixed* (world tour); *The Epic Adventure of Nhamo* (Kiln); *Blood Wedding, The Bacchae* (Royal & Derngate); *As You Like It* (Curve).

On film, his credits include: *The Gates of Vanity*. Ery is also a writer and director, twice awarded a grant by the Arts Council, whose work include: *Motherland* (radio play for The National Archives); *Split/Mixed* (theatre: Royal Exchange/Soho/world festivals inc. Edinburgh Fringe, Hong Kong, New York, San Francisco, Berlin, Clermont-Ferrand); and *Knocking On Heaven's Door* (short: screened at festivals in Cannes, Dallas, Boston).

Kieran Taylor-Ford | Manny

Kieran was born and raised in Camden and is an alumni of both LAMDA and The Brit School.

Keiran's credits include: *For Black Boys Who Considered Suicide When The Hue Gets Too Heavy* (Garrick); *3.2.1* (National Theatre); *Human Nurture* (UK tour); *Holy Sh*t* (Riverside); and *Yerma* (Lyric Hammersmith).

Jamael Westman | Devlin

Born in London, Jamael attended RADA before quickly landing the titular role in the West End production of Lin-Manuel Miranda's musical *Hamilton* which earned him a Laurence Olivier Award Nomination and the Evening Standard Theare Award's Emerging Talent Honour. Since then he has graced the stage in *London Tide* (National Theatre); *Imposter 22, Torn* (Royal Court), *Patriots* (Almeida); *The Lorax*

(Old Vic); and *The White Devil* (Shakespeare's Globe).

His TV credits include: *Get Millie Black*; *The Essex Serpent*; *Anne Boleyn* and *BBW*. His film credits include: *Hedda*; *Good Grief*; *Munch*; *Animals*.

Tom Moutchi | Devlin

TV credits includes: *Criminal Record*; *Plebs: Soldiers of Rome*; *PRU*; *Mood*; *Temple*; and *Famalam*.

Film credits includes: *Gladiator 2*; *Festival of Slaps*; *The Hustle*; and *Warrior*.

Theatre includes: *Barbershop Chronicles* (Roundhouse); and *Twiststorm* (Park).

CREATIVE TEAM

Beru Tessema | Writer

Beru Tessema is an Ethiopian-British writer and director based in London and a graduate of the London Film School and RADA.

Beru's stage play, *Exile in North Weezy*, was shortlisted for the Papatango Playwriting Prize 2020. And his second play, *House of Ife*, directed by Artistic Director Lintette Linton, was produced at the Bush to critical acclaim in 2022. Beru makes work for both stage and screen and is currently developing feature film projects with Film4 and the BBC.

Daniel Bailey | Director

Daniel Bailey is a director, dramaturg and writer for stage and screen. He is currently Associate Artistic Director at the Bush Theatre, London, having joined the team in 2019 alongside Artistic Director Lynette Linton. Prior roles include Associate Director at Birmingham Rep Theatre (after initially joining as part of the Regional Theatre Young Director Scheme), Resident Director at the National Theatre Studio, Associate Artist at Theatre Royal Stratford East, Resident Assistant Director at The Finborough Theatre, and on the Young Vic's directing programme.

His directing work at the Bush Theatre includes Lenny Henry's *August in England* (co-directed with Lynette Linton), *Red Pitch* by Tyrell Williams (Stage Debut Award Winner 2022) and Temi Wilkey's *The High Table* (Stage Debut Award winner 2020). *I Wonder If* (presented with YV Taking Part) had a run at the Young Vic Theatre in late 2022 before going on a community tour, and Daniel was the Creative Associate on the UK Premiere of *Bootycandy* at Gate Theatre. His work at Birmingham Rep includes *Blue Orange, Concubine, Stuff, I Knew You, Abuelo, Jump! We'll Catch You, Made In India/Britain*; and *Exhale*. His previous directing work includes plays with Talawa Theatre Company, Manchester Royal Exchange, New Heritage Theatre, and the New Vic.

His film and TV director credits include: *Dropped* (Mothers Best Child); *On Belonging* (Young Vic); *Malachi* (S.E.D); *Floating on Clouds* (Kingdom Entertainment Group) and *Y.O.L.O. THERAPY* (S.E.D).

Amelia Jane Hankin | Set & Costume Designer

Amelia Jane Hankin trained in Architecture and at the Royal Academy of Dramatic Art then RSC. Amelia has designed a variety of theatre ranging from new writing, devised, touring theatre, immersive, site-specific, community and theatre for young people. Amelia is an Associate Lecturer at the RCA and co-founded the Office for Speculative Spatial Design in 2020.

Design credits include: *Red Pitch* (Soho Place/Bush); *Othello* (Shakespeare's Globe); *Cinderella* (Brixton House); *Mlima's Tale* (Kiln); *Richard III, The Night Before Christmas, Rudolf* (Liverpool Playhouse); *Let The Right One In, Mountains* (Royal Exchange); *Drowntown* (Barbican); *Holes* (Theatre Royal Bury St Edmunds); *The Wave, (This Isn't) A True Story* (Almeida); *Christmas in the*

Sunshine, The Wolf The Duck and The Mouse (Unicorn); *Unknown Rivers* (Hampstead); *Sing Yer Heart Out For The Lads* (Chichester); *One Under* (Graeae); *Blue/Orange* (Birmingham Rep); *The Comedy of Errors* (RSC); *The Fishermen* (Trafalgar Studios); *Gastronomic* (Curious Directive); *PowerPlay* (Historic Royal Palaces); *Good Dog* (UK tour); *Fake It 'Til You Make It* (UK and Australian tour) and *We Are You* (Young Vic).

Studio AJH is based in Hackney, London.

Ali Hunter | Lighting Designer

Ali is a Lighting Designer working across dance, theatre and opera. She trained at RADA and is the Young Associate Lighting Designer for Matthew Bourne's *Romeo and Juliet*. Ali regularly lights for London Contemporary Dance School. She is an Associate Tutor at RADA.

Recent lighting design credits include:

Theatre: *Protest* (Fuel/Imaginate/ Northern Stage); *Notes from a Small Island, Othello, Brief Encounter* (Watermill); *If You Fall, Beautiful Evil Things* (Ad Infinitum at Bristol Old Vic); *Titus Andronicus* (Shakespeare's Globe); *One Off* (Live Theatre); *Samskara* (Yard); *Red Pitch* (Bush); *Orlando, The Marriage of Alice B Toklas and Gertrude Stein* (Jermyn Street); *Small Change* (Both Barrels/ Clapham Omnibus); *Sugar* (Open Clasp, BBC iPlayer); *Don't Forget the Birds, Rattlesnake* (Open Clasp at Live Theatre); *Fix* (Pleasance); *Cash Cow* (Hampstead).

Dance: *Happyendingfication* (Yami Löfvenberg); *Crabs in a Barrel* (Jamaal O'Driscoll); *Inscribed in 'Me'* (Alethia Antonia); *Happy Fathers' Day* (Dani Harris-Walters); *Deuce* (Iona Brie).

Opera: *A Kind Man* (New Palace Opera at Hoxton Hall); *La Nonne Sanglante* (Gothic Opera at Hoxton Hall).

As Associate Lighting Designer: *Lava* (Bush); *The Half God of Rainfall* (Kiln/Birmingham Rep); *Hot Mess* (Candoco Dance).

Duramaney Kamara | Sound Designer & Composer

Duramaney Kamara was born into a family of afro-jazz musicians, becoming infatuated with instruments, live music and production from a young age. His childhood home was filled with reggae, jazz and afro-beat, which continue to influence his composition and music production to this day.

As a child Duramaney performed with his parents in gigs around London, developing a multi-disciplinary talent for playing instruments, his favourite being the trumpet. At six years old he began writing and producing songs on GarageBand and as a teenager was invited to create music in professional studios for artists around London.

Duramaney, aka 'D L K' is also a recording artist and producer who releases music under his indie label Breaking Bread & Boundaries, founded in 2018. He released his debut EP, *F*ck It Let's Move* in 2019, which peaked at #1 in the UK iTunes pre-order charts. He most recently co-produced two tracks on Mostack's latest album, *High Street Kid 2* which made it into the UK Top 40. D L K is set to release more of his own music.

Duramaney is also an actor. He had his stage debut in 2016 at the Almeida in Leo Butler's *Boy* and had his screen debut in 2018 in Idris Elba's feature film *Yardie*. He continues to work as an actor alongside composition and music production.

Gino Ricardo Green | Video Designer

Gino Ricardo Green is a director and video/projection designer. He is co-founder of Black Apron Entertainment.

Credits as Video/Projection Designer include: *Barcelona* (West End); *A Child of Science* (Bristol Old Vic); *Samuel Takes A Break* (The Yard Theatre); *The Flea* (The Yard Theatre); *The Legends of Them* (Hackney Showroom/Brixton House); *Tambo and Bones* (Theatre Royal Stratford East); *August In England*, *Lava* (Bush); *Othello* (National Theatre, Co-Video Designer); *The Ballad of St John's Carpark* (Icon); *Treason: The Musical in Concert* (West End); *Rapture* (Royal Court); *Kabul Goes Pop: Music Television Afghanistan* (Brixton House/ HighTide); *Edge* (NYT); *Lava* (Bush); *Children's Children* (Director of Photography/ Editor – English Touring Theatre); *Beyond the Canon*, *Poor Connection* (RADA); *Sweat* (Donmar Warehouse/West End); *Passages: A Windrush Celebration* (Black Apron at the Royal Court); *Hashtag Lightie* (Arcola); *Lightie* (Projection Designer – Gate).

Credits as Associate Video/ Projection Designer include: *Small Island* (National Theatre); *Get Up, Stand Up! The Bob Marley Musical* (West End); *Be More Chill* (The Other Palace/West End).

Gabrielle Nimo | Movement Director

Gabrielle Nimo is a London-based movement director, teacher and facilitator, who has worked with companies, arts venues and institutions including: Creature Bionics, Talawa Theatre Company, Generation Arts, Guildhall, LAMDA and Arts Ed as former Head of Movement (2020–2022).

Her credits as movement director include: UK Theatre award-winning *Swim, Aunty,Swim!* (Belgrade); *Red Pitch* (Soho Place); *Strategic Love Play* (Paines Plough/Soho); *On The Ropes* (Park); Olivier Award-winning *Sleepova*, *The High Table* (Bush); and *Unknown Rivers* (Hampstead).

Kev McCurdy | Fight Director

Kev is an Equity registered Fight Director and Choreographer of 24 years, professional stage combat tutor of 31 years, Director, Actor and an Action performer. Kev teaches at The Royal Welsh College of Music and Drama and has also taught at universities in Oklahoma and Missouri as well as being a guest instructor on workshops in Norway, Sweden, Finland, Canada, America. Kev is also co-founder of The Academy of Performance Combat.

Theatre includes: *Victoria's Knickers*, *Typical* (Soho); *The Wife of Willesden* (Kiln); *Drifter's Girl*

(Garrick); *Hamlet* (Young Vic); *West Side Story* (Royal Exchange); *The Beauty Queen of Leenane* (Chichester Festival Theatre/Lyric Hammersmith); *The Long Song* (Chichester Festival Theatre); *Grown Ups* (Mischief Theatre, UK tour).

TV and film includes: *The Pact* season 2, *The A List* season 2, *Hollyoaks*, *Set Fire To The Stars*, *John Carter of Mars*, *Season of the Witch*, *Protein*, *Canaries*, *Scopophobia*, *The Lady of Heaven*.

Music videos include: Off Bloom, 'Shut Up and Let Me Walk'; Formation, 'A Friend'; Kayla, 'Mojito'; Circles, 'I See Monstas'; Louis Mattrs, 'War With Heaven'.

Ingrid Mackinnon | Intimacy Director

Theatre credits include: *Dreaming and Drowning* (Bush); *The Choir Boy* (Bristol Old Vic); *Shooting Hedda Gabler* (Rose); *The Effect, Phaedre* (National Theatre); *Tina – The Tina Turner Musical* (Aldwych); Regent's Park Season Associate: Intimacy Support 2023/2022: *La Cage Aux Folles*, *Robin Hood*, *The Tempest*, *Every Leaf A Hallelujah*, *Once On This Island*, *Antigone*, *101 Dalmatians*, *Legally Blonde*, *Carousel*, *Romeo and Juliet*; *The Meaning of Zong* (Barbican/Bristol Old Vic/UK tour); *Blue* (ENO); *Further than the Furthest Thing* (Young Vic); *Trouble in Butetown* (Donmar Warehouse); *Es & Flo* (Wales Millennium Centre/Kiln); *Super High Resolution*, *Typical* (Soho); *Enough of Him* (National Theatre of Scotland); *A Dead Body In Taos* (Fuel); *The Darkest Part of The*

Night, Girl on an Altar (Kiln); Playboy of the West Indies (Birmingham Rep); Moreno (Theatre503); Red Riding Hood (Stratford East); Antigone (Mercury, Colchester); Liminal – Le Gateau Chocolat (King's Head); Liar Heretic Thief (Lyric Hammersmith); Reimagining Cacophony (Almeida); First Encounters: The Merchant of Venice, Kingdom Come (RSC); Josephine (Theatre Royal Bath); #WeAreArrested (Arcola/RSC); The Border (Theatre Centre).

Polly Jerrold | Casting Director

Theatre credits include: Wolves on Road, Paradise Now! (Bush); The Secret Garden, Antigone, Peter Pan, A Tale of Two Cities, Oliver Twist, To Kill a Mockingbird tour, Running Wild tour (Regent's Park Open Air); Romeo and Juliet (Belgrade/Bristol Old Vic); Chasing Hares, The Secretaries (Young Vic); First Touch (Nottingham Playhouse); Life of Pi (Sheffield/West End); Waldo's (Extraordinary Bodies/Bristol Old Vic); Macbeth (ETT); Pretty Shitty Love, Milky Peaks, Celebrated Virgins, Curtain Up, For the Grace of You Go I (Theatr Clwyd); Shandyland (Northern Stage); One Flew Over the Cuckoo's Nest, Tribes (Sheffield); Our Lady of Kibeho, Soul, Merlin, Peter and The Starcatcher (Royal & Derngate); Two Trains Running (ETT/Royal & Derngate); Approaching Empty (Kiln/Tamasha/Live); The Lovely Bones (Royal & Derngate/Birmingham Rep/Northern Stage); All's Well that Ends Well (Shakespeare's Globe); The Caretaker (Bristol Old Vic); The Government Inspector, Tommy,

Our Country's Good (Ramps on the Moon); The Island Nation (Arcola); Brideshead Revisited, A View from the Bridge, Sherlock (York Theatre Royal).

Gurikan Kaur | Voice Coach

Gurkiran Kaur is a voice, accent and dialect coach from London. She holds a BA Drama and Theatre Studies (Royal Holloway), completed actor training (The Bridge Theatre Training Company) and has a MA Voice Studies (The Royal Central School of Speech and Drama). Gurkiran works at a number of drama schools and has coached a number of graduate productions and showcases. Gurkiran is part of The Voice And Speech Teaching Associations' EduCore Leadership Team and serves as a Junior Board Member. Gurkiran honours Ancient practices to approach voice work and believes in serving the people in the space ensuring inclusivity, equity and accessibility.

Credits: Extinct (Stratford East); Queens of Sheba (Soho/Nouveau Riche); NW Trilogy (Kiln); How To Save the Planet When You're a Young Carer and Broke (Boundless); Best of Enemies (Young Vic/Headlong); Chasing Hares (Young Vic/Uncut); I Wonder If (Young Vic); Red Pitch, Favour, The P Word, Paradise Now!, Sleepova, A Playlist For The Revolution, The Cord, The Real Ones (Bush); Lotus Beauty (Hampstead/Tamasha); Henry VIII (Shakespeare's Globe); Offside (Futures Theatre); Marvin's Binoculars, Anansi The Spider (Unicorn); The Climbers (Theatre By The Lake); Finding Home

(Curve); *The Best Exotic Marigold Hotel* (Noël Coward); *Silence* (Donmar Warehouse/Tara); *A Dead Body In Taos* (Fuel); *Unexpected Twist* (Royal & Derngate); *Wuthering Heights* (China Plate); *I Wanna Be Yours* (Melbourne Theatre Company); *The Empress, Falkland Sound* (RSC); *Brassic FM* (Gate); *A Poem For Rabia* (Tarragon Theatre, Toronto); *The Full Monty* (Everyman, Cheltenham /Buxton Opera House); *Good Karma Hospital* (ITV/Tiger Aspect Productions) and *Hotel Portofino* (ITV/PBS/Eagle Eye).

Georgia Wilmot | Costume Supervisor

After graduating with a degree in Interior Design from Liverpool John Moores University Georgia worked on *Misfits* season 3 (Channel 4), and as a costume trainee on *Monroe* (ITV) before deciding that Set Design was something to be explored.

Georgia's set and costume credits include: *The End, Communion, Elephant, Invisible* (Bush); *Covered* (New Heritage Theatre at Paddington Arts Centre); Superdrug's YouTube channel Christmas campaign 2017; *I knew you* (Birmingham Rep); *days of significance* (Questors).

In 2018 Georgia had the opportunity to create concept designs and illustrations for Designer Tim McQuillen-Wright for Secret Cinema's *Blade Runner*. In 2021 Georgia designed sets for the Bush Theatre's Project 2036: *Pawn* by Devon Muller, *One Day* by QianEr Jin and *LimBo* by Latekid. In August 2021 Georgia

returned to Bush to design the set and costume for the Young Company's first main house performance *Back Up!*, devised and directed by Katie Greenall.

Georgia illustrated the first children's book from *The adventures of* series, as well as working as a digital design content creator for *My Trauma, My Healing* with Simone Powderly. During the last year, Georgia has written and illustrated her first children's book and created a range of illustrations as part of a diversity and inclusion campaign.

Lisa Hood | Production Manager

Lisa trained in Theatre Arts at Middlesex University.

Selected production management credits include: *Macbeth* (ETT/ Lyric Hammersmith); *Red Speedo* (Orange Tree); *Anna Hibiscus' Song* (Utopia UK tour); *Trials and Passions of Unfamous Women* (LIFT Festival, Brixton House); *Northanger Abbey* (UK venues); *Macbeth* – as associate (ETT European tour); *Merchant of Venice 1936* – as associate (West End); *Dreaming and Drowning* (Bush); *Woodhill* (LUNG UK tour); *The Flying Dutchman* (Opera Up Close, UK tour); *My Uncle is Not Pablo Escobar* (Brixton House); *An Octoroon* – as Stage Manager (Orange Tree); *Jess and Joe Forever* – as Stage Manager (UK tour).

Tayla Hunter | Company Stage Manager

Tayla Hunter is a 2022 Stage manager graduate from the Royal Central School of Speech and Drama. She previously worked on two shows at the Bush Theatre during their 2022 season: *The P Word* (Olivier Award winner) and *Paradise Now* (Olivier Award nominee) and is now making her official debut as company stage manager on *Wolves on Road*. Tayla is particularly passionate about representing and telling stories from the black community. In addition to her dedication to theatre, she is eager to expand her skills and explore opportunities within the film and television industry, with aspirations to progress to show calling, seeking to gain as much experience and skill as possible along the way.

Assistant Stage Manager credits: *Superhumans – Minding the Gap Youth Projec*t (Kiln); *Black Superhero* (Royal Court); *Paradise Now!*, *The P Word* (Bush); *Lotus Beauty* (Hampstead); *A Place for We* (Park).

Assistant Stage Manager/BOOK COVER Credits: *Slave Play* (Noel Coward); *The Big Life* (Stratford East) ;and *Beneatha's Place* (Young Vic Theatre).

Company Stage Manager Credits: *Best Fit* (Peckham Fringe) and *Imaginary Natural Beings* (VAULT Festival).

Bush Theatre

We make theatre for London. Now.

For over 50 years the Bush Theatre has been a world-famous home for new plays and an internationally renowned champion of playwrights.

Combining ambitious artistic programming with meaningful community engagement work and industry leading talent development schemes, the Bush Theatre champions and supports unheard voices to develop the artists and audiences of the future.

Since opening in 1972 the Bush has produced more than 500 ground-breaking premieres of new plays, developing an enviable reputation for its acclaimed productions nationally and internationally.

They have nurtured the careers of writers including James Graham, Lucy Kirkwood, Temi Wilkey, Jonathan Harvey and Jack Thorne. Recent successes include Tyrell Williams' *Red Pitch*, Benedict Lombe's *Shifters*, and Arinzé Kene's *Misty*. The Bush has won over 100 awards including the Olivier Award for Outstanding Achievement in Affliate Theatre for the past four years for Richard Gadd's *Baby Reindeer*, Igor Memic's *Old Bridge*, Waleed Akhtar's *The P Word* and Matilda Feyiṣayọ Ibini's *Sleepova*.

Located in the renovated old library on Uxbridge Road in the heart of Shepherd's Bush, the Bush Theatre continues to create a space where all communities can be part of its future and call the theatre home.

'The place to go for ground-breaking work as diverse as its audiences' EVENING STANDARD

bushtheatre.co.uk
@bushtheatre

h&f
hammersmith & fulham

ARTS COUNCIL
ENGLAND

Supported by
ARTS COUNCIL
ENGLAND

Artistic Director	Lynette Linton
Executive Director	Mimi Findlay
Associate Artistic Director	Daniel Bailey
Deputy Executive Director	Angela Wachner
Development & Marketing Assistant	Nicima Abdi
Development Officer	Laura Aiton
Head of Marketing	Shannon Clarke
Head of Development	Jocelyn Cox
Associate Dramaturg	Titilola Dawudu
Finance Assistant	Lauren Francis
Resident Director & Young Company Director	Katie Greenall
Technical & Buildings Manager	Jamie Haigh
Assistant Venue Manager	Rae Harm
Head of Finance	Neil Harris
Marketing Officer	Laela Henley-Rowe
Associate Producer	Nikita Karia
Community Assistant	Joanne Leung
Senior Producer	Oscar Owen
Assistant Venue Manager	Simon Pilling
Senior Technician	John Pullig
Event Sales Manager & Technician	Charlie Sadler
Venue Manager (Theatre)	Ade Seriki
Press Manager	Martin Shippen
Community Producer	Holly Smith
Literary & Producing Assistant	Laetitia Somè
Marketing Manager	Ed Theakston
Assistant Venue Manager (Box Office)	Robin Wilks
Theatre Administrator & Executive Assistant	Chloe Wilson
Café Bar Manager	Wayne Wilson

DUTY MANAGERS
Sara Dawood, Molly Elson, Thomas Ingram, Madeleine Simpson-Kent & Anna-May Wood.

VENUE SUPERVISORS
Antony Baker, Addy Caulder-James, Stephanie Cremona, Emma Chatel, Zea Hilland, Nzuzi Malemda, Roy Mas, Jacob Meier & Louis Nicholson.

VENUE ASSISTANTS
Javine Aduganfi, Doridan Bavangila, Charlotte Binns, Will Byam-Shaw, Pyerre Clarke, Daniel Fesoom, Matias Hailu, Bo Leandro, Maya Li Preti, Ishani McGuire, Khy Matinez, April Miller, Ed Mendoza, Carys Murray, Chana Nardone, Jennifer Okolo, James Robertson, Ali Shah & Nefertari Williams.

BOARD OF TRUSTEES
Uzma Hasan (Chair), Mark Dakin, Kim Evans, Keerthi Kollimada, Lynette Linton, Anthony Marraccino, Jim Marshall, Rajiv Nathwani, Kwame Owusu, Stephen Pidcock, Catherine Score & Cllr Mercy Umeh.

Bush Theatre, 7 Uxbridge Road, London W12 8LJ
Box Office: 020 8743 5050 | Administration: 020 8743 3584
Email: info@bushtheatre.co.uk | bushtheatre.co.uk

Alternative Theatre Company Ltd
The Bush Theatre is a Registered Charity
and a company limited by guarantee.
Registered in England no. 1221968 Charity no. 270080

THANK YOU

Our supporters make our work possible. Together, we're evolving the canon and creating a bolder, more diverse, and representative future for British theatre. We're so grateful to you all.

MAJOR DONORS
Charles Holloway OBE
Jim & Michelle Gibson
Georgia Oetker
Cathy & Tim Score
Susie Simkins
Jack Thorne
Gianni & Michael Alen-Buckley

SHOOTING STARS
Jim & Michelle Gibson
Cathy & Tim Score
Susie Simkins

LONE STARS
Jax & Julian Bull
Clyde Cooper
Adam Kenwright
Anthony Marraccino &
Mariela Manso
Jim Marshall
Georgia Oetker

HANDFUL OF STARS
Charlie Bigham
Judy Bollinger
David des Jardins
Sue Fletcher
Thea Guest
Elizabeth Jack
Simon & Katherine
Johnson
Joanna Kennedy
Garry & Lorna Lawrence
Phyllida Lloyd & Kate
Pakenham
Vivienne Lukey
Aditya Mittal
Sam & Jim Murgatroyd
Mark & Anne Paterson

Martha Plimpton
Nick & Annie Reid
Bhagat Sharma
Joe Tinston & Amelia
Knott
Dame Emma Thompson

RISING STARS
Elizabeth Beebe
Martin Blackburn
David Brooks
Catharine Browne
Anthony Chantry
Lauren Clancy
Richard & Sarah Clarke
Caroline Clasen
Susan Cuff
Matthew Cushen
Anne-Hélène and Rafaël
Biosse Duplan
Austin Erwin
Kim Evans
Mimi Findlay
Jack Gordon
Hugh & Sarah Grootenhuis
Sarah Harrison
Uzma Hasan
Lesley Hill & Russ Shaw
Davina & Malcolm
Judelson
Mike Lewis
Lynette Linton
Michael McCoy
Judy Mellor
Caro Millington
Rajiv Nathwani
Yoana Nenova
Stephen Pidcock
Miguel & Valeri Ramos
Handal
Karen & John Seal

James St. Ville KC
Jan Topham
Kit & Anthony van Tulleken
Evanna White
Ben Yeoh

CORPORATE SPONSORS
Biznography
Casting Pictures Ltd.
Nick Hern Books
S&P Global
The Agency

TRUSTS & FOUNDATIONS
Backstage Trust
Buffini Chao Foundation
Christina Smith Foundation
Daisy Trust
Esmée Fairbairn Foundation
The Foyle Foundation
Garfield Weston Foundation
Garrick Charitable Trust
Hammersmith United
Charities
The Harold Hyam Wingate
Foundation
Idlewild Trust
Jerwood Foundation
Martin Bowley Charitable
Trust
Noël Coward Foundation
The Thistle Trust

**And all the donors
who wish to remain
anonymous.**

If you are interested in finding out how to be involved, please visit **bushtheatre.co.uk/support-us** email **development@bushtheatre.co.uk** or call **020 8743 3584**.

TAMASHA

For over 30 years, Tamasha has been a dedicated home for both emerging and established Global Majority artists.

A powerhouse of new writing, talent development and digital innovation, we platform and invest in stories that celebrate our rich shared histories and cultures. Proudly both artist and audience driven, we're disrupting, dismantling, and inspiring through bold and imaginative storytelling, providing a place to explore our lived experiences and unique perspectives.

We support theatre makers in gaining the skills, knowledge and creative community to create innovative, new work. Our Developing Artists Programme includes masterclasses, showcases, training programmes and networking opportunities, informed by and responsive to the evolving demands of the creative industries.

We collaborate with partners to commission and produce an artistic programme interweaving live and digital productions, such as audio dramas, walking adventures, magazine-style podcasts and annual touring productions. All staged within and beyond traditional spaces.

Productions over the company's history have included *East is East* by Ayub Khan Din, *Blood* by Emteaz Hussain, *Approaching Empty* by Ishy Din, *Does My Bomb Look Big In This?* by Nyla Levy, *I Wanna Be Yours* by Zia Ahmed, *10 Nights* by Shahid Iqbal Khan, *Made In India* and *Lotus Beauty* by Satinder Chohan, *Hakawatis* by Hannah Khalil, *STARS* by Mojisola Adebayo and *Great Expectations* by Tanika Gupta.

WOLVES ON ROAD

Beru Tessema

'The burden of poverty isn't just that you don't always have the things you need; it's the feeling of being embarrassed every day of your life, and you'd do anything to lift that burden.'

Jay-Z

4

Characters

MANNY, *Emmanuel, twenty-one, a mixed-heritage Londoner*
FEVAN, *his mother, forty, an Ethiopian-British chef*
ABDUL, *his best friend, twenty-one, Somali-British*
MARKOS, *forty-seven, an Ethiopian immigrant*
DEVLIN, *thirties, Black British. A crypto entrepreneur*

Note on Text

A forward slash (/) indicates the start of overlapping dialogue or
an indication of leaving no space between the dialogue. Where
there is no punctuation, it indicates a continuation of the
character's thought, intention or action.

*This text went to press before the end of rehearsals and so may
differ slightly from the play as performed.*

ACT ONE

Scene One

Spring 2021.

The Three Flats, Bow, East London. Canary Wharf and the financial buildings of the City are visible in the distance yet out of reach, like another country on another shore.

MANNY is in the living room. Boxes of counterfeit Louis Vuitton bags and other fake designer goods are everywhere.

MANNY's phone rings. He ignores the call. He opens the boxes and carefully inspects the items. He checks his appearance in the mirror. His phone rings again. He dismisses the call.

MANNY spruces himself up as he goes into performance mode and starts a live-stream on Instagram. It is clear from the way he talks and moves that he is a true hustler.

MANNY. Yo! What you sayin' people? It's your booooooy from Bow E3! The Drip is here! New garms just dropped! Exclusive, high-end shit straight from the factories of Pa-ri! Grrrrrrrrrrrrrrrrraaaaaaaaah! Yo! I'm getting gassed! Look at dis! See dis? This ain't juss drip. This *is* drrrrrrriiiiippp!

MANNY finds various angles to film the bags on his phone.

Louis V people! You can reach your boy right here @DripInTheHood. I got Gucci bags for the mandem too, Versace creps, some Louis belts, 'n' remember if you spend anything above a bill you get a free delivery as well yeah.

Notifications and likes stream in. MANNY tries to address each of them.

Yes, Kisha! Wha' you sayin'? Dis one? This retails for about two grand innit, but we're doin' a deal on this for five bills. Two bills? You takin' the piss! You ain't gonna find prices like this *nowhere*. Trust me. (*To another follower.*) Man like

Devanté! Big man! LV bag for your queen, yeah? Which one? Of course, it comes in the box it came in, obviously. What do you think / dis is?

A stream of DMs light up his phone. MANNY *lays out another set of bags on the floor for the live-stream.*

This ain't that 'made in China' shit you lot get down Roman Road Market. This the real deal! *Authentic!* / See this?

FEVAN *enters from work carrying shopping, giggling and flirting on the phone with a man we will come to know as* MARKOS. *She puts her shopping down.*

FEVAN (*on the phone*)....you put the phone down first. No, you. Go on, then. No, you, go on... okay... huh... I'll see you when you get here... Yeah, he's here... / I know... I'm sorry...

MANNY. Ah, Mum, man! I'm / working!

FEVAN (*still on the phone*). Don't worry... okay? It will be fine. I'm always here, okay? Bye / babe...

MANNY (*still live-streaming*). You can order right here / @DripInTheHood

FEVAN. Ah, Manny, what's / all this?!

MANNY. Or juss DM me, but all dis gonna go quick, so place your order / asap!

MANNY *takes pictures of the merchandise and uploads them to his Insta.*

FEVAN. He was waiting for / you

MANNY. Who? /

FEVAN. What do you mean who? Markos. He's waiting for you, and here you are, filling the flat with this rubbish / again!

MANNY. It ain't rubbish, Mum, it's / LV.

FEVAN. I don't care what it is. Why weren't you answering / when

MANNY. I was busy / Mum

FEVAN. He's busy / too.

MANNY (*excited*). Yo, yo Mum, Mum, I got you / somethin'

FEVAN. Didn't you say you'd meet / him?

MANNY. Mum, one sec, close your / eyes

FEVAN. Are you / listenin'?

MANNY. Close your eyes, Mum!

FEVAN. Do you see what he's going through right / now?

MANNY. Mum, please!

FEVAN. Okay, fine! (*Under her breath.*) Fuck sakes…

> FEVAN *closes her eyes and holds her arms out.* MANNY *rushes to choose the most expensive-looking Louis Vuitton bag and places it in her hands.*

MANNY. Boom.

FEVAN (*opening her eyes*). What's this?

MANNY. Try it.

FEVAN (*trying it on her shoulders*). I got plenty of bags, Manny, I don't need you spending / your

MANNY. What do you mean? You think I'll let my mumzie be on road with no swag? C'mon!

FEVAN. No swag? What, / me?

MANNY. I don't mean it like that! See? Propa suits you! They hand-craft these in Paris you know. It's the real deal, Mum. Surplus from the Louis Vuitton factories / innit.

FEVAN. I wish you would have called or texted / him.

MANNY. Nah, I literally juss come back from gettin' tha sickest deal. It was this warehouse that supplies Selfridges 'n' dem places there innit. They all wanna partner up 'n' that, coz they can see I'm trying to make high-quality fashion actually affordable for everyone… Wait. One / sec…

MANNY *grabs a standing mirror and moves around to show* FEVAN *how she looks with the bag.*

Jheeeeeeeeeeeeze! Look at you! G'wan Mumzie! Braaaappp brrraaapppp / brrraaapppp!

FEVAN. Manny?

MANNY. Best-dressed chef, Mummy! Look at that! It looks good on you, you know! It / looks good!

FEVAN (*ignoring him*). Who wants to partner / up?

MANNY. Look Mum! See how like, elegant you look? Propa chic, ya get me. You know what they call that bag? They call it the *Croissant Bag* coz of the shape. It's a classic. Thought you'd like it. An iconic bag for an iconic chef!

FEVAN. This is a lot Manny. I don't want you getting burnt again /

MANNY. I'm not gonna get burnt, Mum. I know what I'm doin'. This is the one; trust me.

Beat.

FEVAN. You had him worried.

MANNY. What, he's tryin' to son man now, yeah? I'm a big man out here ya / know!

FEVAN. Just be kind to him, Manny, that's all I'm / asking!

MANNY. Once sec Mum, I juss need to finish takin' these / pictures.

FEVAN. You're fussing about designer bags when our country's burnin' / up.

MANNY. Why you speaking like that?

FEVAN. Like what?

MANNY. Like him, like Markos / innit.

FEVAN. What? Is he the only one that's allowed to have an opinion?

MANNY. Mum, you ain't never been back so don't try it!

FEVAN. War's kicked off in our country Manny. Don't be ignorant about / it.

MANNY. Ah, Mum man, you're getting all deep; I don't wanna talk about all that stuff right now.

FEVAN. Next time, make an effort with him, okay?

MANNY. What does he want? Your hand in marriage / or something?

FEVAN. Don't be / stupid!

MANNY. I'm out here hustlin' all day, I ain't got time to sit and / chat!

FEVAN. Hustling? His son's gone missing, and he's still showing up for you! Don't embarrass / me.

MANNY (*taking more pictures*). Ah, Mum man, you're steppin' on my garms! Do you know what that's / worth?

FEVAN. We need to be there for him right now. He hasn't heard from his boy since this war started.

MANNY. Okay, fine, Mum, let me just finish doing / this

FEVAN. How much did you spend on all this?

MANNY. Nah, don't watch that – inventory / innit.

FEVAN. Where did you get the money / from?

MANNY. Borrowed it / still.

FEVAN. Borrowed it? From / who?

MANNY. From a friend innit. It's / calm.

FEVAN. Don't be borrowing money you can't pay back. I'm not gonna pay off your debts / again

MANNY. Why you always bringin' that up? It / was just

FEVAN. I'm tellin' you now – I'm not gonna do it again. That money was supposed to be for my restaurant.

MANNY. I'll pay you back. I told / you.

FEVAN. I keep sayin' – you can come work with me or get yourself a proper job. / You're

MANNY. Propa job? This is my / job

FEVAN. Last month it was 'mobile barbers', and now it's designer / bags?

MANNY. See? You don't get it, Mum, this is Drip In Tha Hood. I'm building a brand /

FEVAN. A brand?

MANNY. Yeah. A brand. Do you know the amount of man that's makin' millions from doin' this ting / online?

FEVAN. What ting / online?

MANNY. Brands innit. There's man out there building empires / 'n' shit!

FEVAN. You're tryin' to run before you can walk. It takes time to build something meaningful. If you wanna get into fashion, go to school and learn about it, or find an apprenticeship son, / just

MANNY (*kissing his teeth, busying himself with taking more pictures*). Ah, Mum, man, allow me with the / lectures.

FEVAN. Don't be kissing your teeth at me. You're a grown man now, and I'm telling you, if you wanna get anywhere in life, you can't cut corners.

MANNY. I / know.

FEVAN. And don't be tryin' to chat to me about hustling – I'm the original hustler /

MANNY. Oh my dayz / man!

FEVAN. Yeah, I've been hustlin' since you were born. I took no short cuts. You listenin'? It took me all this time, but when people taste my food, they / know.

MANNY. Ha! (*Under his breath.*) It ain't gonna take me that long!

FEVAN. What?

MANNY. Nothing.

FEVAN. Afropean fusion like / you.

MANNY. Afropean yeah? Sounds / bougie.

FEVAN. That's why I can say it with my chest; and when I get my place, it's going to be a game-changer round here.

MANNY. Yeah, that's easy. It's only Ali's kebab shop and that flippin' Chicken Cottage round here.

FEVAN. Why you being like that?

MANNY. I'm juss sayin' I'm not a dreamer, Mum. I'm a doer.

FEVAN (*wounded*). What, you think I'm just dreaming?

MANNY. Mum, how long you been talking about opening your own place?

FEVAN. Nothing worthwhile comes / easy.

MANNY. That's what broke people say. You have to switch up your mindset, Mum. Swear / down!

FEVAN (*stung by* MANNY's *comment*). Anyway, he's coming round now; you can apologise to him / when

MANNY. Apologise?

FEVAN. Yes, apologise.

MANNY. Are you joking?

FEVAN. Even with everything he's going through, he's still there for you /

MANNY. You know you can do better, Mum.

FEVAN. Stop it /

MANNY. I'm juss bein' real. The bredda's been here for years, 'n' he can't even speak English properly.

FEVAN. You think speaking English 'properly', whatever that means – is the measure of a person?

MANNY. Nah, he's been here for time, 'n' he's still movin' like he's fresh off the boat, Mum, I ain't gonna / lie

FEVAN. Give him a chance 'n' you might learn something.

MANNY. Ah, Mum, man! You keep stepping on my garms! You're messin' them up! I need to take these / pictures!

FEVAN. He's gonna be here soon. I can't have this place looking like this, / it's

MANNY. What? Here?

FEVAN. Yes, remember? You were supposed to walk down together and we / were

MANNY. This brea man, he's always comin' / here.

FEVAN. Stop.

MANNY. What?

FEVAN. This. Sulking. You're not a teenager any more, Manny. You have to let me have my own life, too, you / know.

MANNY. Why don't you lot go out? What, is he low on funds again or / something?

FEVAN. He's supportin' a lot of people back home. He don't have the luxury to be spending money on himself /

MANNY. But does he spend money on you?

FEVAN. Manny /

MANNY. Exactly. See? You can do better Mum.

FEVAN. We're just gonna have some dinner and maybe watch a film. You're welcome to / join.

MANNY. Nah, you're takin' the piss, man's tryin' to work / 'n'

FEVAN. What, is that a problem?

MANNY. How long you gonna be?

FEVAN. I'll text you when he leaves.

MANNY (*under his breath*). Fuck / sakes!

FEVAN. No one's forcing you to be here, Manny.

Beat.

You should have your own space. A flatshare or something? That's what most people your age are doing /

MANNY. Yeah, I know. Don't worry, innit. I'll be gone / soon.

FEVAN. I was bringing you up and working full-time when
I was your age – on my own in that little bedsit /

MANNY. Yeah, I know I was there /

FEVAN. I'm just saying take the leap, and you'll find your feet.
I was always so scared back then. But we still made it fine,
didn't we? You never wanted for anything, did you?

MANNY. Always wanted my own room.

FEVAN. I know, but we made it work here, didn't we? We were
always happy here, weren't / we?

MANNY. Trust me, if you were my age now with a likel yut,
you'd still be in that bedsit. You wouldn't have no council
flat to be drawing man back / to.

FEVAN. What?!

MANNY. Sorry.

FEVAN. 'Drawing man back to'?!

MANNY. I didn't mean / to

FEVAN (*snapping*). Don't talk to me like that!

MANNY. I was joking!

FEVAN. Why can't you be happy for me?

MANNY. I am happy for you. I juss don't wanna be on road all
night when I got work in the morning.

FEVAN. What work?

MANNY. I gotta take a few of these samples to a couple of
outlets first / thing.

FEVAN. Right.

MANNY. It's just a few boxes anyway. The freshie ain't gonna
mind / is he?

FEVAN. He's not a 'freshie'; he's got a / name.

MANNY. Do you reckon he'd want to buy some / Gucci loafers?

FEVAN. It's illegal. All this crap you keep dragging in / here.

MANNY. Oh my days! How's it illegal?

FEVAN. Manny, selling counterfeit products is / illegal.

MANNY. Thass your opinion. 'N' this ain't no / counterfeit.

FEVAN. It's not my / opinion –

MANNY. You're sayin' it's counterfeit / but

FEVAN. It's the / law.

MANNY. What? I can't even store a couple of boxes in my
    own / yard?!

FEVAN. Get your *own* yard and you can store as many boxes as
    you like in / there.

MANNY. Yeah, I will.

FEVAN. Good.

MANNY. I'm gonna have one of them penthouses up there in
    Canary Wharf soon. Watch.

FEVAN. Who's the dreamer now?

Scene Two

Late afternoon, the following day.

MANNY *is pushing a trolley loaded with his boxes full of his
designer goods. He is frustrated, trying to make a phone call
but getting no answers. His friend* ABDUL *is walking beside
him, distracted by his phone's constant notifications.* ABDUL *is
glued to his Binance trading app as he talks to* MANNY.

MANNY. Nah, they've fucked me, bruv! They've fully fuckin'
    fucked me! Everyone's sayin' this shit is all fake bruv!

    MANNY *tries calling again. Still no answer. He is panicking.*

ABDUL. / What?

MANNY. I been all over flippin' Shoreditch 'n' all up 'n' down
    Brick Lane bro, and none of these pagans want any of / this!

ABDUL (*to himself*). Ah, / yes!

MANNY. What?

ABDUL. Ten per cent surge on Bitcoin! Grrrrrrrrrraaaaaaaah!!! / Yes!

MANNY. Bro, you even fuckin' listenin'?

ABDUL (*still distracted*). Fam, you juss got finessed by dem Romanian donnies innit. Three racks for this shit? You got shegged bowy! Propa bumped!

MANNY. Nah, I'm fucked! I borrowed that money from Sneaks innit, 'n' he's already tryin' to get on to man about paying him / back 'n' that

ABDUL. Wait. What? Sneaks from Red Flats? Bro, you crazy?

MANNY. Nah it was supposed to be a quick ting / innit.

ABDUL. Bro, why didn't you come to me first

MANNY. I did. I texted you bare times 'n' you straight aired / man!

ABDUL. I was working bruv. You should have emailed / me

MANNY. Went on like you didn't even receive the messages 'n' ting

ABDUL. You were askin' for some reckless sums when I told you I was literally gettin' wiped out, and then you go to / Sneaks?!

MANNY. You didn't even reply / bruv

ABDUL. Nah, I been tryin' to level-up with this tradin' ting, but Wallahi I would have lent you the / money

MANNY (*anxious*). Nah… this brea… He's sayin' he's gonna send a couple of man with Rambos to my yard if I don't have his money / ready.

ABDUL. Ah bro man! Bro dem breddas are sadistic. See that video they posted, cheffin' up that yut in Mile End?

MANNY. I had pay dem Romainian breddas / innit

ABDUL. Sneaks is legit a psycho – you know that? That brea's got a fuckin' hole where his soul should be. Watch. I bet he's gonna make you go country 'n' fuckin' rinse you!

MANNY. Nah, fuck that. I juss need / time.

MANNY *desperately goes to make another phone call.*

ABDUL (*still processing*). Yo, I still can't believe you went to fuckin' Sneaks!

MANNY. Fuck man! Fuck! Bruv, I feel sick!

ABDUL. See if you can sort out a Klarna ting him or something / bro.

MANNY. Nah, he wants the full amount, bruv. Keeps textin' me. I donno where I'm gonna get that three grand from. I've rinsed all my overdrafts payin' off that fuckin' loan from the mobile barber / ting

ABDUL. 'You turn your losses into assets when you learn from them.'

MANNY. What?

ABDUL. Warren Buffett!

MANNY. Shut up, man! That's some dumb shit to say. An L is still an L innit, and swear down, I can't take any more bruv. Thass all I been taking. Straight Ls to the chest 'n' I'm fuckin' done with / it.

ABDUL (*distracted by the charts on his phone*). I'm tellin' you now bro, if you came to me with them three racks, bruv, trust me, we woulda made money on / that

MANNY. Is that supposed to help me?

ABDUL. What?

MANNY. You sayin' / that?

ABDUL. One sec. (*To himself as he types a message.*) W-A-G-M-I, my guy!

MANNY. What?!

ABDUL. Nah, some brea is juss buggin' out on dis crypto Telegram group ting / I'm on

MANNY. W-A-G-M-I?

ABDUL. Wagmi – means we're gonna make it /

MANNY. You 'n' your crypto / chat

ABDUL. Fam, you should be puttin' all this hustle into making some real money. I keep tellin' you, bro, this is the year of crypto. (*Showing him the charts.*) Look! My portfolio's gone up twenty per cent, bro! Twenty per cent! It's not just Bitcoin, fam. Dogecoin, Solana, and Ripple, bare coins are killin' it right now.

MANNY. Crypto ain't real money /

ABDUL. What you chattin' 'bout? I made eight bills off it the other / day

MANNY. Eight bills?

ABDUL. Yes bro, eight bills in one day. The price of Bitcoin's been going off the fuckin' chain and bringing all these other coins up with it.

MANNY. Weren't you losing bare money on that / though?

ABDUL. Crypto is mad volatile, you get it? (*Showing him the chart on his phone.*) See? Always moving and that. (*Distracted by a tweet.*) Rah, wait… one sec… bare people getting gassed about Shiba Inu on / Twitter.

MANNY (*looking at* ABDUL*'s phone over his shoulder*). What, *you* actually got a Bitcoin fam?

ABDUL. Nah, it's juss a fraction, innit. One Bitcoin is like sixty racks now, fam. Imagine. Satoshis. People think you need bare money to invest in Bitcoin, but you don't. You can literally invest whatever you have 'n' still make dough from it. Look at this fam. My portfolio's fuckin' mooned!

MANNY. Mooned?

ABDUL. My money's gone up over five hundred per cent on some of these / coins!

MANNY. Rah /

ABDUL. That's what I'm tryin' to tell / you

MANNY. Five hundred / per cent?

ABDUL (*showing* MANNY *his charts*). Look, Dogecoin bruv. This how mad this ting is; flippin' Elon Musk tweets Tesla will accept payments in Doge, and this coin's gone to the fuckin' moon. I've already made two racks on dis, fam, but if it dips, I'm fucked; that's why you have to stay vigilant coz this shit moves / quick!

MANNY (*looking at the chart on* ABDUL*'s phone*). This shit looks propa complicated, / bruv.

ABDUL. Nah, I can show you innit. I'm juss learning too, fam.

MANNY. How do you know when to make all these moves / though?

ABDUL. You juss have to stay on the charts 'n' use your instincts, innit. Why you think I'm up all night on Twitter, 'n' WhatsApp, on flippin' Telegram groups 'n' everything? Thass how I'm making my money bro. I'm preeing what all these cryptoheads are on from here to flippin' America, ya get me? Man's gettin' price alerts every day so I know when to buy 'n' when to sell. You have to be a student of the game out here. Most man can't hack it coz it's a twenty-four-seven hustle bro; you have to stay plugged in if you wanna get to The Bag. Certain nights I ain't even sleepin'; I'm up all night, hustlin' on these charts / bro.

MANNY. That's mad!

ABDUL. Some of these coins been makin' mad gains since we come out of lockdown fam, turning bare people into fuckin' millionaires 'n' shit.

MANNY. Swear / down?

ABDUL. Yeah, bro, you know Devlin?

MANNY. Devlin?

ABDUL. Devlin from Malmesbury Estate.

MANNY. Oh yeah, that bredda with the YouTube / channel?

ABDUL. Yeah, him, I wouldn't be surprised if *he's* touchin' a mill.

MANNY. Nah. What? You reckon?

ABDUL. He brought his mum her council flat time ago, innit. All cash bruv. That brea's been making big moves from day. He was the first one around here to jump on this crypto ting 'n' now look at him. He's lookin' after his family 'n' livin' good.

MANNY. He's got bare jarrin' videos on YouTube, though. Man's all on there screamin' 'bout crypto like it's some new religion!

ABDUL. Lockdown, bruv. He got bare followers in lockdown innit, coz mandem clocked there's money to be made.

MANNY. He's still living in endz innit?

ABDUL. Yeah fam, he's got one of them penthouses in that converted church by Vicky Park.

MANNY. Fam, them yards in that building are worth like over a millie ya / know!

ABDUL. Thass what I'm tryin' to tell / you

MANNY. He's got a yard *there* bruv? Damn. Bro, I need to jump on this crypto ting asap! I ain't / joking

ABDUL. But bro, you have to be patient. You can't see it as sum overnight ting /

MANNY. I juss always hear about mandem gettin' scammed 'n' / whatnot.

ABDUL starts rolling a spliff.

ABDUL. If you're dumb, yeah. Dumb breas are always gonna get scammed, don't matter if it's crypto or the Stock Market, bro. That's how these bankers keep gettin' rich; they're wolves innit. Wolves eating the sheep. Get me? That's how it's always been, and it ain't gonna change. But if you know what you're doin' and you know where to look; you can get to The Bag 'n' secure it, fam; you juss need to be smart about it. You get me: you have to be a wolf out here, not a sheep.

Beat.

What, how much you got left?

MANNY. I just got about five bills left fam. 'N' that's everything. That's all I got to my name now ya get me.

ABDUL. Five bills, yeah? Bro, that's more than enough to start with / still.

MANNY. I dunno, man, I need to get this dickhead off my back innit; he's tryin' to say he'll start uppin' it by a hundred pounds a day if I don't pay him *now*.

ABDUL. Fam, if you're on it, we can try makin' some of that money back.

MANNY. You reckon?

ABDUL. It's a gamble though, ya get me, I ain't gonna lie. I'm juss saying it's a bull run right now so the chances are, if we play it right, we can make some of that money back.

Beat.

What you sayin'? You on it, yeah?

Scene Three

Late that evening. MANNY *is on his sofa bed, engrossed on his laptop. His phone is on a stand, on a FaceTime call with* ABDUL. *They've been at this for hours.*

MANNY *gets a stream of text messages and checks it. He is worried.*

MANNY. This fuckin' guy man! He don't stop!

ABDUL. You alright?

MANNY. Sneaks innit. He's sayin' I have to go Coventry to deliver some shit for him / bruv

ABDUL. Rah, he's got you goin' country already? That's / peak!

MANNY. This guy's a snake. I told him I don't even drive 'n' he's tellin' me to get the / train!

ABDUL. Fuck him, man. What can you see now?

MANNY. My Binance account innit, it's up and runnin' now. Propa long. Askin' man for bare verifications 'n' / shit.

ABDUL. You typed in my referral code, / yeah?

MANNY. He's got some youngers shottin' outta some crackhead's yard up there, and thinks I'm gonna take food up there for him on some bait route, ya know! I ain't never even been to Cov!

ABDUL. Bruv man, focus!

MANNY. Yeah, I'm on / it

MANNY gets another text message. He checks it.

ABDUL. Let's pattern dis ting 'n' you can pay him back. Simple.

MANNY. Now he's sayin' I don't have to pay the hundred-pound-a-day interest if I do the delivery.

ABDUL. Bro, that sounds like a set-up. I'd stay away from that shit if I was / you.

MANNY. You're sayin' dat like I have a / choice!

ABDUL. See this? Bull flags like these are propa rare. I'm telling you bro, we need to jump on this Shiba Inu ting / asap!!

MANNY's distracted by the sound of a man singing outside and a woman laughing.

MANNY. Thass what I'm tryna do innit. Wait, what do mean bull / flags?

ABDUL. The chart fam. See how Shiba's going up like flags on a pole. (*Hyped.*) Yo! This is / crazy!

FEVAN enters, followed by MARKOS, who is dressed in his TfL bus driver's uniform. FEVAN is a little tipsy, but MARKOS is drunk, singing an old Amharic song, and falls into the space while clumsily dancing. FEVAN giggles, enjoying MARKOS's song and helping him up, but quickly gestures for him to shush when she sees MANNY.

FEVAN. Ah, I thought you were out, son.

MANNY (*annoyed at the interruption*). Fuck / sake man!

FEVAN. Manny! Dawit called! He called, / and he's alright!

MARKOS (*tipsy*). Ah! Emmanuel! Hey men, I wait for you, and you disappear men! I / thought

MANNY (*trying to focus on his charts*). I was / busy

FEVAN (*giggling*). I'm so sorry son. I'm so sorry. He's / just

MARKOS. Praise God! Praise God for our sons! For all our sons! Eh! *Elelelelelelelelelele!*

FEVAN (*trying to shush him*). Markos, Markos, / Markos…

MANNY. Oh my dayz / man!

FEVAN (*to* MANNY). Sorry, we just heard the news / and

MARKOS. God is good, son! I thought I had lost him, but He heard / me!

   MARKOS *breaks out into another song of worship. He takes up all the space and fills it with an intoxicated sense of joy.*

MANNY. Mum?!

FEVAN (*trying to usher* MARKOS *to the bedroom*). Shhhh! You're gonna wake the whole / building!

   MARKOS *tries to dance with* FEVAN *around the tight space.* FEVAN *is tickled by this but is still trying to guide* MARKOS *to the bedroom.* MANNY *watches, fuming.*

ABDUL. Yo, / fam?

FEVAN. Come on Markos! You're / drunk!

MARKOS. I'm not drunk, Fevan, I'm just happy! I am blessed eh? I am / blessed!

FEVAN (*privately to* MARKOS). Let's get you to bed /

ABDUL. Fam, you there?

MANNY (*snapping*). Mum / man!

FEVAN. Sorry, sorry. It's just such great news today. He's had one too many.

MANNY. Can't you see we're / workin'?!

ABDUL. / Yo…

   MARKOS *is still singing and is joyfully drunk.*

FEVAN *ushers* MARKOS *to the bedroom and closes the door behind her.*

FEVAN (*off; playfully to* MARKOS). Hey! Listen, I'm gonna have to kick you out if you don't behave!

We hear their merry laughter, music and MARKOS*'s singing.* MANNY *stares after them at the closed door. He is clearly pissed off.*

MANNY. Yeah, I'm here, I can hear / you.

ABDUL. You alright?

MANNY. Nah, this guy innit, comin' to my yard all drunk 'n' / shit

ABDUL. What Markos?

MANNY. Yo, what do I do / now?

ABDUL. Twitter's buzzin' 'bout dis coin Shiba Inu!

MANNY. Bro?

ABDUL (*showing* MANNY *his screen*). Juss follow what I'm doin' innit. You already deposited your money in there, yeah?

MANNY. Nah, / fam

ABDUL. Bro? You takin' the piss? How you out here tryin' to trade without no / peas?

MANNY. Fam, I'm tellin' you now, if I lose this money. Swear down / bro

ABDUL. Eh, lissen. Lissen yeah, in dis ting you have to invest money to make money. That's just / standard.

MANNY. Nah, / I'm juss

ABDUL (*snapping*). You want to do this ting or / not?

MANNY. Oi, watch your tone / bruv!

ABDUL. Big-man tings yeah. Stop fuckin' around 'n' let's pattern this / then!

MANNY. Nah, don't chat to me like I'm sum dickhead innit, I've deposited my funds. Now / what?

ABDUL. You ain't gonna learn nothin' bein' touchy.

> MANNY *hears sounds coming from* FEVAN*'s bedroom.*
> *He tries to block it out. It sounds like* FEVAN *and* MARKOS
> *quietly having sex and giggling. This is too much for*
> MANNY.

> Boom. I'ma start with five bills, straight. Shiba Inu's lookin'
> like it's going to the fuckin' moon. Mad hype on this coin
> right now. How much you putting in?

MANNY (*rattled by* FEVAN *and* MARKOS*'s sounds*). I'm juss
gonna start with a hundred quid innit, see what happens /

> *The noises* FEVAN *and* MARKOS *are making get louder.*

ABDUL. Whoa! This why everyone's been gettin' hyped! This
is it bruv! It's already surgin', you see that?

MANNY. Fuck it; actually, I'll put in five bills as / well.

ABDUL. Five bills? You / sure?

MANNY. I ain't gonna do no fuckin' county lines for Sneaks
bruv, I ain't goin' jail for him, ya / get me.

ABDUL. Rah, you're a gangsta fam. Man's puttin' it all on the
line ya / know!

MANNY. I'm tellin' you bro, this better work, I'm fuckin' dead
if it / don't

ABDUL. We got this; stop stressin'. Go to the spot markets tab,
not futures /

MANNY. Futures?

ABDUL. Don't worry 'bout that. I don't want you gettin' spun
on your first trade /

MANNY. Ain't gonna lie fam, I'm baffed, propa / baffed

ABDUL (*making the purchase*). Watch 'n' learn bro, man's
a hustler out here. Open the Ethereum and British Pounds
market. If you're puttin' five bills in there, use the buy option
to buy nought point two Ethereum for five hundred pounds,
ya / get me?

MANNY *hears* MARKOS *drunkenly stumble to the toilet and heavily urinate.* MANNY *is pissed off.*

MANNY (*scared*). Nought point two? Is that all they give you for five bills?!

ABDUL. Fam, lissen yeah, you ain't gonna make money by juss holdin' on to it. That's a broke way of thinking, ya / understand?

MANNY *gets another text message.*

MANNY. He's sayin' for me to go up there this Friday.

ABDUL. Fam, ignore him. We're gonna level-up tonight if this surge carries on. You got your Ethereum, yeah?

MANNY. Nah, wait, I'm doin' it now innit.

MANNY *tensely makes the purchase after some hesitation. He makes an animal-like sound when he makes the purchase order.*

Okay, cool, so what do I do now?

ABDUL. Boom. Cool. Can you see where it says buy SHIB? That's Shiba Inu.

MANNY. / Yeah

ABDUL. Where it says the price bro, we're gonna use all our Ethereum so put in nought point two there. The amount we can get for that is fifty million SHIB.

MANNY. Fifty million SHIB? Rah, this crypto ting's a mazzaline fam!

ABDUL. No one's seen a surge like this for a long time. Trust me, we're going to the fuckin' moon with this! When you're ready, just click buy SHIB.

MANNY. Fam, I'm trustin' you innit. I'm trustin' you with my life right now. You know that, don't you?

ABDUL. People are sayin' it's gonna go up times a thousand! Do you know what that means bruv?

MANNY. Thousand times the profit.

ABDUL. It already had some mad surge a few months ago;
    made bare man some serious dough, fam! We can't miss out
    on gettin' to The Bag this time, ya get me?

> ABDUL *makes the purchase and* MANNY *follows him,
> making another more intense animal sound as he does it.*

> Done?

MANNY. Done.

ABDUL. Whoosh.

MANNY. Ain't gonna lie. This a propa buzz / fam

ABDUL. It is innit? Truss, this shit gets addictive. Why you
    think I'm off-grid 'n' on dis ting all night!

> *Setting up the order,* MANNY *following him.*

> Okay boom, so what we gonna do now is create a sell order
> in the same / market

MANNY. Wait, I don't get / that

ABDUL. When the price hits, we're gonna sell this coin back at
    ten times the price – just to be safe.

MANNY. What? For real? And make ten times the amount?!

ABDUL. Yeah /

MANNY. Five bags each?

ABDUL. Yeah bro, but it will only execute the order
    automatically if the price reaches this target we're setting
    now. We got this bruv, trust me. You doin' it?

MANNY. Yeah, done. What do we do now fam?

> *Beat.*

ABDUL. We wait innit.

Scene Three B

Hours later, MANNY *struggles to stay awake. The crypto market is constantly moving.* ABDUL *appears on the screen.* MANNY *is in a dream state, navigating strange charts and figures.*

Scene Four

The following morning. MANNY *is asleep, sat on the sofa, still in the clothes from the previous night.*

FEVAN (*offstage*). Morning son. You awake? We alright to come in?

> MANNY *wakes up, startled.* FEVAN *enters from her bedroom, followed by* MARKOS, *who is still dressed in his TfL bus driver's uniform but this time looks well put together.*

MARKOS. Ah, Emmanuel! I'm sorry about last night, son. I think I made a fool of myself, / eh?

MANNY (*sharply*). Bruv, it's Manny, yeah?

FEVAN. Manny! /

MANNY. What?

FEVAN. What did I say to / you?

MARKOS. Sorry, / Manny

FEVAN (*going into the kitchen*). 'God is with us.' That's what your name means, yeah? Listen, I gave you a big name ya know. You need to put some respek on / it!

MANNY. Oh my dayz, / man!

MARKOS. Sorry we disturbed you last night. It's just, Dawit... he called me... from Sudan! My son Dawit. Can you believe this? I don't hear from him all these months, and when I hear his voice, my heart just... I could just breathe again, you / know

FEVAN (*from the kitchen*). Markos! This teff / is amazing!

MANNY (*scrambling to log back into Binance*). I'm happy for you.

MARKOS. I need coffee. You know I am lightweight. Two beers, and I'm gone! Do you want some?

MANNY. Nah, I'm alright.

MARKOS. He was supposed to go to Addis Ababa University. Addis is safe, but he would rather go to the desert and the / sea

MANNY. Yo Markos man, I need to work ya / know

MARKOS. Ah, forgive me, my head is still spinning. I'm still delirious from hearing his voice, you know…

   MARKOS *goes to make coffee. He still wants to interact with* MANNY, *but* MANNY *is too busy scrambling around trying to set up his charts again.* FEVAN *excitedly comes in with a freshly made single injera and offers some to* MARKOS.

FEVAN. What do you think?

MARKOS. Wow wow wow / wow wow

FEVAN (*offering some to* MANNY). Son?

   MANNY *is glued to his screen and freaking out that he can't access his money.*

MARKOS (*to* MANNY). Eh men, try your mother's injera! It's made with teff from Lalibela where I grow up! One of the wonders of the world. I will take you there one day. You and your mother, and you can see it. They say an army of angels carved the churches out of the rocks there one night.

FEVAN. Army of angels, yeah? I like that!

MARKOS. That's what they say.

FEVAN. Nah, you're a smooth talker, Markos. You got that voice, ya know… /

MANNY. Yo, this is good, Mum! This is propa good, you done well.

FEVAN. You think?

MARKOS. Yes, it's delicious. (*To* MANNY.) Hey men, they are calling this teff a superfood now!

MANNY (*back on his screen*). Is it?

MARKOS (*to* FEVAN). You got it perfect. This is exactly how it tastes back home! / Exactly!

FEVAN. Ah I'm glad. It's that teff man. I'm gonna make the rest when I get there. Serve it to them fresh /

MARKOS. You are giving those white boys the real deal, eh? They're lucky!

FEVAN. Listen, if they give me that pop-up spot, do you know how crazy that will be?!

MANNY (*quietly at the screen*). What the fuck / man, c'mon!

MARKOS. Of course, they'll let you have it. After everything you've given to that place, it's the least they can / do.

FEVAN. You know what, them lot see me on my grind every day in that kitchen. You know I low-key run that place innit? Trust me, that's all me in there! I'm not even joking if they don't give me this spot I'm / done. Done.

MARKOS. They will give you that spot! Ooooooohhhhweeeee! Those white boys are going to taste all this spice and not know what hit / them!

FEVAN (*seeing the time*). Shit! I better get ready.

MANNY *calls* ABDUL *on FaceTime as he sets up his charts.*

(*To* MANNY.) Oi, don't let that stuff with the bags get you down. Chin up!

MARKOS. Ah, this is a new computer game or / something?

MANNY (*to* MARKOS). What do you mean computer game? You think I'm sum likel / yut?

FEVAN. Oi, why you being rude? /

MARKOS (*to* FEVAN). It's okay. Can I make you coffee?

FEVAN. Please. But in my to-go cup. I'm so fuckin' late now! (*Exiting to get ready.*)

MARKOS (*to* MANNY). You sure you don't want any?

MANNY *is too stressed out over the charts on his screen and does not reply.*

FEVAN (*to* MANNY). Oi /

MARKOS. No, it's fine. I know how passionate young men are about their computer / games.

MANNY (*to* MARKOS). Yo, why you keep calling it a computer game? Ain't you seen charts / before?

MARKOS. Ah, charts! You are mathematician like me, eh?

MANNY (*panicking as he calls* ABDUL *again*). Where the fuck's this / guy man?!

FEVAN (*coming back in. To* MARKOS). You should finish that. Don't you like it?

MARKOS (*eating*). Ah! You spoil me!

FEVAN (*bringing in more food for* MARKOS *to taste*). What do you reckon?

MARKOS (*eating*). Ooooooooh!

FEVAN. That's what I'm talking about! Give people something different. Food should be an experience. Kitfo with awazae, collard greens, just for them to start with. It's good innit?

MARKOS. This is amazing! Wow wow / wow!

MANNY. Yo, Mum, do you want me to try that as well?

FEVAN. Might be a bit too spicy for you.

MANNY. Nah, let me try it!

FEVAN *gives him some.*

It's good

MARKOS. She is a great chef, your mum! I keep telling her she needs her own place now, not a pop-up.

FEVAN. A pop-up will do just fine for now.

> FEVAN *exits again, getting ready.* MARKOS *pours the coffee into* FEVAN*'s to-go cup and into his own mug.*

MANNY (*trying to navigate the charts on his laptop*). Fuck man! / Fuck!

FEVAN (*offstage to* MANNY). Hey, what's the matter with / you?

MANNY. This fucking / thing!

FEVAN. Listen, I paid good money for that laptop! Don't be dashin' it around like / that!

MANNY. I need to concentrate, Mum; I'm tryin' to trade!

MARKOS. Ah, trading? This is trading?

> MANNY *does not respond to* MARKOS. MARKOS *quietly drinks his coffee, watching* MANNY *frantically trying to figure out the charts.*

MANNY (*putting on a YouTube Binance tutorial as he calls* ABDUL *again*). Pick up your / phone man!

FEVAN (*offstage to* MARKOS). I'll be ready to go in five minutes. You can walk me to the bus / stop.

MANNY. Come on man, pick up your fucking / phone bruv!!

FEVAN (*offstage to* MARKOS). Can you find something to pack the food in?

MARKOS (*shouting back to* FEVAN). / Okay.

> MARKOS *looks around the kitchen, finds some large bags, and carefully packs the containers of food into it.*

ABDUL (*finally answering*). Bro!

MANNY. Bro man, where the fuck you been?!

ABDUL. Fam! Have you seen this?

MANNY. What?

ABDUL. Bro! What do you mean what? Check your Ethereum wallet bro!

MANNY. What? What am I looking / at?

ABDUL. Show me your / screen

MANNY. It's an old laptop, fam it don't let me share my / screen

ABDUL. Juss use your phone then innit. Show me what you're lookin' at.

MANNY *uses his phone to show* ABDUL *his screen.*

You see where it says wallet fam?

MANNY *still doesn't know what he's looking at.*

See that?!

MANNY. What?

ABDUL. Bro! The market increased twelvefold in the last eight hours! Can you see? We could have made so much more bro, but it processed our order at ten / innit

MANNY. Wait. What, are you sayin' we just made the five bags?

ABDUL. You got two Ethereum there bro; that's five grand each!

MANNY. Yooooooo??

ABDUL. It went to the fuckin' moon!

MANNY (*still in disbelief*). Oh my God bruv! Oh my God!!! Yo! Abz! Is this us, bruv? Is this us??

ABDUL. What did I tell / you?

MANNY. Oh my days, bruv! Yo! This is mad!

ABDUL. It's still surgin' bro; we need to jump on it now!

MANNY. Five bags each! Ten grand! Are you mad??

ABDUL *and* MANNY *wildly celebrate.* MANNY *is triumphant, leaping around the room, roaring with victory.* MARKOS *watches the boys ecstatically celebrate.*

ABDUL. They reckon this is gonna carry on for another day bro. This is the one innit!

MANNY (*suddenly returning to his computer*). Bro? Bro? Bro...

FEVAN (*offstage*). Emmanuel!

MANNY. How do I take it out? Bro? How do I take it out?

ABDUL. You wanna quit now?

MANNY. Yeah, fam, exit. Exit now, / innit!

ABDUL. Bro, we can double this, I'm tellin' / you!

MANNY. Nah, I need to take this money out now bro. How do you do / it?

FEVAN (*offstage*). Manny?!

ABDUL. Fam, it's still an upward movement; with all this money, we can have mad leverage if we go on futures!

MANNY. What do you mean futures?

ABDUL. Just means we're bettin' on the future price on this ting, and we already know it's surgin' innit. It's a no-brainer /

MANNY. Leverage using what though?

ABDUL. What do you think bro? We got five bags each sittin' there. We need to make this money work for us /

MANNY. What all of it?

ABDUL. Not all of it bro, but I reckon we can even make fifty bags on this if we ten-ex it on futures. You should see what people are / makin'

MANNY. Fifty grand? What! That's / nuts!

MARKOS. Fifty? Wow wow wow / wow wow!

ABDUL. No one's seen this kind of surge bro! It's one of them rare times to juss fuckin' rinse it! Rago!

MANNY. I'm fuckin' buzzing! Fifty racks, ya know! Grrrrrrrraaaaaaaaaah!!!

ABDUL. Grrrrrrrrraaaaaaaahhhhh!!!! Awoooooooooooooooo!!!!! (*More howling.*)

FEVAN (*offstage*). What's / going on?

ABDUL. Wolves now bro! We're wolves now bro, innit? What did I tell you?

MANNY. Wolves out here / bro!

ABDUL. Wolves on road ya get / me!

MANNY *and* ABDUL *ecstatically howl like wolves in a wild celebration.*

MANNY. Bro! What? How do you do the futures ting on / dis?

ABDUL. Juss follow what I'm doin' innit, we'll start small first, ya get / me.

MANNY. *Small* bro. Start small. I ain't lookin' to lose none a this money!

FEVAN *enters, finally ready to leave.*

FEVAN. Emmanuel, I'm talking to you: what on earth is going on?

MARKOS. I think your son just made ten thousand pounds.

Scene Five

MARKOS *walks* FEVAN *to the bus stop. She carries the bag containing the food she has prepared and a couple of larger containers in her hands.*

FEVAN. What's up?

MARKOS. Huh?

FEVAN. You've gone somewhere else.

MARKOS. It's just… you know I was sending that money for his education, not for him to pay some smugglers and then lie to me about it. He didn't even tell his grandparents. He's made them sick with worry.

FEVAN. At least you got through to him; that's all that matters.

MARKOS. I always hoped he'd be one of the ones who would build our country, not run away from it, but he would rather chase the life he sees on the internet here.

FEVAN. You can't blame him. It's crazy what's going on over there.

MARKOS (*going to carry the box for her*). Sorry, I am being rude. Let me get / that.

FEVAN. I got it.

MARKOS. No, no, no, it's okay, let me get it for you.

She stops at an empty, dilapidated storefront shop that has seen better days.

FEVAN. Look. It's *still* empty, ya know!

MARKOS. Covid's been a curse on a lot of these small businesses.

FEVAN. The amount of loan applications I had to do, and now look at it. It just sits there boarded up and fallin' / apart.

MARKOS. I see it every day on my bus route. All these places boarded up.

FEVAN. I used to leave Manny here some nights when I had to go to work. Mrs Khan would let him perch at the counter there, and he'd do his colouring; she'd even let him serve customers sometimes. He loved it. Standing there on a stool cos he was too small to reach the / till

MARKOS. Ah! The boy was a businessman from the / start!

FEVAN. I'd come back knackered. I was taking any work I could back then; Ricardo /

MARKOS. Manny's…? /

FEVAN. Yeah, Manny's dad took everything, / and

MARKOS. I'm sorry / to

FEVAN. What can you do? He was an addict.

MARKOS. Still… /

FEVAN. When we moved here, it was a fresh start, away from him, just me and Manny. When I'd get back from work those nights, he'd be upstairs in that flat, where the Khans lived, fed and watching TV, always fed…

MARKOS. They sound like good people. I always believe it takes a village to raise a child. My boy Dawit had his grandparents, cousins, uncles, and everyone there is like family. You'll see it. I will take you when this war is over.

FEVAN. I've always wanted to go back. Go and find my folks. I probably got brothers and sisters out there I don't even know about.

MARKOS. We'll go.

Beat.

FEVAN. Can you imagine?

MARKOS. Huh?

FEVAN. What I could do with a place like this now? Kitchen full of aunties from all over. That's what I'd have. All those aunties who can cook better than a lot of chefs out there but can't get work, imagine what they could make if they had a / chance?

MARKOS. Yes, / yes, that

FEVAN. A proper down-to-earth restaurant, but celebrating the culture and the story of the people around here, you know what I mean? Where everyone can come together and eat and dance /

MARKOS. Wow, wow, wow, wow, this is what people need right now! /

FEVAN. A community kitchen table. That's what I'd want it to be.

MARKOS. Community kitchen table! Yes, I love it!

FEVAN. There's this famous Ethiopian chef with the same name as you, Marcus Samuelsson; you know him?

MARKOS. Yes, yes, he has a restaurant in Addis. I know him!

FEVAN. His restaurant in Harlem is all about that. Community, music and good food. Imagine having something like that here?

MARKOS. You can do it. You are, how you say… not sous chef but masterchef! You can do it!

FEVAN. I been tryin' ta do it!

MARKOS. No, it's true. You can do it. I believe in / you!

FEVAN. I know I can, but try tellin' that to the banks! But…
  you're sweet…

MARKOS. Ah! Me? No, you flatter / me!

FEVAN. No, you are… you're beautiful…

MARKOS. Oooooooh no no no no no / no no!

FEVAN. What?

MARKOS. It's strange for me. A woman calling me beautiful. /
  It's…

FEVAN. Look at you! Black man blushin'!

MARKOS (*touching his chest*). You make this open.

FEVAN (*pointing to her legs*). You make these open!

MARKOS. What?! Eh! Fevan! Ssssh!

FEVAN. I tried to ssssh last night, but you were doin' *that* thing.

MARKOS. Sorry?!

FEVAN. Sorry for what?

MARKOS. I was trying to say… I really enjoy being with you.

FEVAN. I like it…

MARKOS. Which?

FEVAN. When you express yourself like that.

MARKOS. Ah, I'm still learning. I want to be a good man and
  a good father.

FEVAN. I want him to have that.

MARKOS. Who?

FEVAN. Manny. I want him to have someone like you.

MARKOS. He's a smart boy. Already making all that money!
  Did you see?

FEVAN. Ricardo would make that kind of money as quickly as he'd lose it.

MARKOS. It's trading.

FEVAN. Trading what, though? Is that even real – that ten grand he made?

Beat.

He wants to take short cuts like his dad. He's got that same desperation, that lost look. He needs someone like you to guide him.

MARKOS. I'm not sure he likes me very much.

FEVAN. He just needs more time with you.

MARKOS. I'm here for him.

FEVAN. It's always just been me and him, you know…

MARKOS. I know.

They arrive at the bus stop. FEVAN *is pensive.*

FEVAN. Here we are.

Beat.

Thanks.

MARKOS. For what?

FEVAN. For walking with me.

MARKOS. Come on! Of course. We are… you know… we are…

Beat.

FEVAN. I'm just saying. It's nice.

MARKOS. Anytime.

FEVAN. It's here.

MARKOS. Yes.

FEVAN. Let me know if you hear anything from Dawit.

MARKOS. Yes –

The bus arrives, and FEVAN *goes to get on it.*

I will be praying for you. I know you'll get it.

FEVAN *playfully crosses her fingers in the air.*

Beat.

I love you.

Beat.

MARKOS *watches the bus drive off.*

Scene Six

ABDUL *is on edge, stressed out, as he trades on his tablet in the dilapidated playground on the estate.* MANNY, *dressed in an ill-fitting flashy suit, enters, breathlessly running like he has just escaped a hunt, carrying a tote bag and wearing a hat with a 'Digital Gold Exchange' logo on it. He scans the area for danger as he catches his breath.*

ABDUL. Rah, what? Man got all dressed up 'n' shit to go community / centre?!

MANNY. That dickhead's tryin' to send man to Coventry bruv! You see that Punto speedin' off? That was him innit. I come out the community centre, and one of his boys tried chasin' man down Roman Road innit. One waste-yut ya know! I woulda thumped him in his head if I weren't wearin' my suit bruv! Truss, he's lucky ya know!

ABDUL. Oi, Sneaks ain't gonna stop till you go country for him, bruv!

MANNY (*incensed*). I always see that Punto parked outside my yard / now

ABDUL. Nah, going counch is a mad ting bruv! Imagine you get arrested? That would be a wrap. Or if one of them crackheads up there rob you? Sneaks is the kind of brea that will set you up!

MANNY. Yeah, well, I coulda had him off my back by / now!

ABDUL. But whatever you do, bruv, never plug them tings there; once you plug it for him, means he's got you, fam!

MANNY. Shut up! I'm in this shit now coz of you / innit!

ABDUL. What?

MANNY. You 'n' your dumb trades, bruv. I had five racks in the bag, 'n' you fucked it!

ABDUL. Yo, who you chattin' / to?

MANNY. You. I'm chattin' to you, bruv. We lost ten bags!

ABDUL. ICP token was at an all-time / high.

MANNY. All-time high? Then it crashed. Like / Shib

ABDUL. Everyone lost, bruv; you're not the only / one.

MANNY. Yeah, you should have pulled out when I said. Let me show / you

   MANNY *takes* ABDUL*'s tablet.*

ABDUL. Oi, what you doin'? Don't touch my shit! I'm tryin' ta fuckin' / work!

MANNY. How much you make? See, this why you need / *education*!

ABDUL. What the fuck you / doin'?

MANNY. Oi, get off me, bruv. I juss wanna see if you made back my / dough

ABDUL. Nah, that's a vile man, give it back / man!

MANNY. Shut up!

ABDUL. What? Oi bruv! Oi!

MANNY. And what?! What?!

They fight. It's messy and emotional, more like wrestling than throwing punches. They are soon tired and stop, exhausted and breathing heavily on the floor.

Yo? Yo, Abz you alright?

ABDUL. Nah, don't ever try steppin' to me like that, bro. I'll fuckin' knock you out next time /

MANNY. Fam, it's juss this ting with Sneaks. It's fuckin' with my head, ya get / me.

ABDUL. Don't take it out on me then, innit. Tryin' to take man for a dickhead ya / know

MANNY. Nah, bro… I'm sorry… what, we bless, yeah? We bless?

ABDUL. Just get back on your grind 'n' pay him back. Simple. It's not that deep, bruv.

Beat.

Yo, but you shouldn't be rollin' around endz dressed like that, ya get me.

MANNY. This Armani, bro; what you chattin' 'bout! See, that's your problem: zero swag.

ABDUL *dusts himself off and gets back to his trades.*

Yo, I'm telling you, you should have reached Devlin's ting today. Digital Gold Exchange, ya know! Them man are makin' big moves out here! Truss. I'm thinkin' this DGX ting could be the one! It could be a big opportunity for us / bro.

ABDUL. DGX? It's not even a propa crypto exchange / is it?

MANNY. I was all chattin' to Devlin after the ting yeah and fam – you know they're recruitin' new marketing associates 'n' that? He remembers us man still, and was sayin' we should / apply

ABDUL. Marketing associates? For / what?

MANNY. DGX, bruv. What do you think? We can get a share of it, fam. Big moves, ya get me? He's gonna do another seminar at the community centre next week, bro.

ABDUL. Nah, sounds like a hype ting.

MANNY. He's talkin' 'bout gettin' all the mandem round here to have… what was it… propa digital financial literacy 'n' that. If we had that, yeah, if we had that, we wouldn't have lost all that money, innit?

> ABDUL *is stung by the comment.* MANNY *takes items out of the tote bag and throws a DGX brochure to* ABDUL.

> Read it. They're lookin' to make this ting the biggest crypto exchange in the / world!

ABDUL. Look at you! Comin' like a cryptovangelist already, / yeah?

MANNY. Bro, they even have their own token. We can get one DGX Token for every person we bring in. Think about that; one DGX Token is worth a hundred 'n' forty quid!

ABDUL. I'm a trader, I ain't no fuckin' door-to-door salesman /

MANNY. Yeah, you're a trader with no education, fam; that's the surest way to keep takin' Ls.

> MANNY *shows* ABDUL *the Digital Gold Exchange app on his phone.*

> The app is sick! It's bare… intuitive 'n' that, and fam, look, you can get educational packages on it, too. Sick, / innit?

ABDUL. The app's mad / basic

MANNY. That's the point, fam. It's about accessibility innit. Look how much I've made already! It's easy to use. Look: boom boom boom! See that? Stackin' two bills in one day! Man's comin' like some greazy A-one trader! Ya see me?

ABDUL. What? A couple of bills? That's nothing.

MANNY. I ain't even explainin' it to you properly, bro; you should juss come see for yourself. I told Devlin about you innit. Told him you were a self-taught trader, and he was propa impressed. He's looking for people like us to join his / team.

ABDUL. Ah, fam / man

MANNY. You need to fix up first / though

ABDUL. Fix up?

MANNY. I ain't gonna be introducing you looking like this /

ABDUL. Like what?

MANNY. Fam, Devlin's a serious guy, ya know. You need to show that you can move like a greazy trader too, ya get / me?

ABDUL. What?

MANNY. You can't be lookin' like some ghetto yut with a do-rag 'n' shit /

ABDUL. I don't care / man

MANNY (*showing* ABDUL *an image of Hamza on his phone*). Look, see? Hamza. The founder 'n' CEO of DGX bruv. See his drip?

ABDUL. That ain't no drip, fam; he looks like a fake DJ / Kalid!

MANNY. One of the *Time*'s One Hundred most influential people in the world this year bro! They're calling him a crypto visionary / fam!

ABDUL. It's just another crypto exchange, ain't nothing visionary about what he is / doing.

MANNY. You don't get it. I'm tellin' you these man are lookin' to change the world bro, 'n' we can get in on the ground floor 'n' be part of / it.

ABDUL. I don't wanna change the world, I juss wanna make / money.

MANNY. See? You're a pagan!

ABDUL. I'm juss being / real.

MANNY. Nah, you're a negative brea ya know that? Always on some negative vibes. You ain't gonna get nowhere thinking like that.

ABDUL. The whole ting looks a bit cultish, innit.

MANNY. Cultish?

ABDUL. Yeah, fam, cultish.

MANNY. People said the same thing about Apple / fam

ABDUL. DGX ain't no / Apple bro

MANNY. Come see for yourself. This ting is a movement fam!

MANNY *shows* ABDUL *Devlin's Instagram account.*

Look. Mad / innit?

ABDUL. Rah, is that Devlin yeah? What? Is that him with Kevin Hart?

MANNY. Yeah bro. Bare celebrities in America are on this / ting

ABDUL. What! He's got a Lambo / yeah?

MANNY. Bruv, you should have seen what he was driving today. Some sick Rari / bruv

ABDUL. Swear down?

MANNY. Yeah bro, sum classic / ting

ABDUL. Dubai looks sick fam. He's doin' these talks everywhere / boy!

MANNY. Look at his yard. Whoosh. Mad view of Vicky / Park!

ABDUL. What you stalkin' man now?

MANNY. Nah, I've seen these yards on Rightmove, fam. I know what they look like inside / innit

ABDUL. Binance killer, yeah? Is that what they are calling it?

MANNY. Definitely! I reckon it will / be.

ABDUL. Message him.

MANNY. What? Now?

ABDUL. Yeah, see what he's sayin'. See if he has any insights on the market / today

MANNY. Come on, man. It don't work like / that.

ABDUL. Bruv, juss ask him what to trade today, see what he's / sayin'?

MANNY *is hesitant.*

MANNY. I don't have his number.

ABDUL. Voicenote him on Insta.

MANNY. And say what?

ABDUL. Speech him innit. Bro, juss do it. Stop wasting / time!

MANNY. Me wastin' time? You take the piss, bruv!

ABDUL. Do it then!

> MANNY *kisses his teeth at* ABDUL, *then goes into hustler mode when he starts recording a voicenote for Devlin.*

MANNY. Yo Devlin... It's Manny. We spoke earlier; I'm here with my bredrin I was tellin' you about... I juss wanna say we're ready to work for you 'n' that... it's just we lost money on a trade innit, so we can't pay for any training packages at the minute, but if you give us an opportunity, I promise we won't let you down, man. Let me know if that's possible. Me and my boy Abz are experienced in sales and know the area really well; we're hungry, and if you give us a chance, trust me, we'll be the best marketing associates you've got round here. Let me know. Thanks. Love.

ABDUL. Ah, bro that was cringe / man

MANNY. What?

ABDUL. You worded that like some beg friend!

MANNY. How am I beggin' it?

ABDUL. You heard yourself bruv? Propa bum lickin'!

MANNY. Shut up!

ABDUL. Like a thirsty yut dawg, like a / simp!

MANNY. See, this why you don't get no jobs bruv. You don't know how to hustle.

ABDUL. What you chattin' about?! I been hustlin' since I was a little yut / fam

MANNY. Yeah, sellin' sweets 'n' Capri-Sun in the playground ain't / hustlin'

ABDUL. Nah, I had to get on my grind from early / bruv

MANNY. What grind? The only jobs you've ever had was that stall on Roman Road Market 'n' then Footlocker, and you got fired from / both!

ABDUL. Yeah, I was flippin' twelve or thirteen when I started at that market stall, bro. I didn't know what I was doin' / innit.

MANNY. I used to beg you to get me a job on that stall, and you used to go on propa stush /

ABDUL. You know what it was, bro; I woulda brung you in, but that brea that ran that stall was fuckin' racist, fam. Usta call man a black paki 'n' shit, 'n' I juss used to take it on the chin 'n' carry on workin' ca I was the man of the house and had ta look after my brothers innit. They were tryin' to deport my pops them times there still.

MANNY *is distracted by his phone.*

Anyhow, I see that brea on road, fam, I will slap him. How can you talk to a little yut like / that?

MANNY *gets a notification on his phone.*

MANNY. Bro, bro, bro, it's him. It's him, bruv! He replied!

Beat.

ABDUL. What's he sayin'?

MANNY *plays the voicenote.*

DEVLIN (*voicenote*). Emmanuel, yeah? Hold your proper name, king. Don't be choppin' and changing it na mean? Say it with your chest. Don't be comin' with that shaky voice. What, so you man juss wanna join as marketing associates off the bat? It don't work like that big man. You need to get your education first. You should join the Foundation Programme, and trust me, you'll do a lot better with your trades. The Foundation is free for everyone.

MANNY. Ah, pissed /

ABDUL. What?

MANNY. He's tryin' to take man for some fresh donny ya know. This Foundation ting he's chattin' about is for these uncles and aunties who don't know nothing about crypto.

ABDUL. See, I told you this was a long / ting.

MANNY. Wait. Shush bruv. Shush. (*Recording a voicenote again with a deeper voice*.) Yo Devlin, thanks for getting back to me, man. Nah, me and my boy been propa studyin' the whole crypto ting and trust me we have a solid foundation already. I told you we made ten bags, innit. Ten thousand pounds in juss one trade. We know what we're doin', and we're using DGX now; we both think it's the best platform out here 'n' we wanna help you expand it. Trust me, we're DGX heads, we believe in it one hundred per cent, ya get me. I just wanna ask, though… do you reckon we can get a trial run as marketing associates? Give us a week, and let us show you what we can do.

MANNY *sends the voicenote*.

ABDUL. Allow it, bro.

MANNY. Was my voice shaky?

ABDUL. Bruv, stop beggin' / it

MANNY. Fam, this brea is Head of UK Outreach 'n' he's chattin' to us! He knows my name! He remembers /

ABDUL. Nah, deep it; why they chargin' people bare money for these educational packages?

MANNY. What, you think it should be free? These man are runnin' a / business.

ABDUL. No one round here can afford to pay for this / shit.

MANNY. Okay, how much do people round here pay for all these useless degrees that give them nothing? Look at you bruv. You went uni thinkin' you made it, but you're back in endz hustlin' like me.

MANNY *gets another notification*.

ABDUL. Shut up, man; I just went for one year, bruv. Why do you think I dropped out? Coz I clocked was long, innit.

MANNY. Yeah, but you still got some hefty debt. See, you got finessed!

ABDUL. Nah, that shit gets written off after thirty years /
anyway so

MANNY. Wait, shush, it's him...

MANNY *eagerly plays the message*.

DEVLIN (*laughing for a moment*). Yeah, you know what, let's
do that. You remind me of how I was back in the day still, so
I'm gonna give you lot a chance. One week, and let's see
how many active users you man can register. We'll send you
lot a bit more info, but we're introducin' the new upgraded
international money-transfer feature now. So make sure
you're focusin' on registerin' people who're already using
services like Western Union and MoneyGram 'n' them kind
of platforms there, yeah? There's a lot of people in the endz
sending money back home 'n' getting ripped off. We can
help them. If you register, let's say, fifty people as users in
one week, then you can start as associates. It's just a trial run
though, a probation innit... let's see how you lot do.

MANNY *quickly records a response*.

MANNY. Ah D man thank you! Thank you so much!

ABDUL (*quietly to* MANNY; *embarrassed by his overt
enthusiasm*). Bro, chill / man

MANNY. Yo, we won't let you down. We got you! Thank you,
man. Thank you. Bye... bye... bye...

Finishes recoding the message and sends it.

ABDUL. Fifty people?

MANNY (*elated*). Bro! Bro! Bro! See? Speeched it! What?!
Marketing associates, yeah! Woi! C'mon! What you sayin'?

ABDUL. I dunno, man.

MANNY. Bro, fifty people. That's all we have to register.

ABDUL. That's a lot of people, bro.

MANNY. Fam, look how many people there are on the estate.
We can do this, bruv. Trust me!

Scene Seven

Fevan's kitchen. FEVAN *is setting up an impressive spread of Ethiopian food on the table.* MARKOS, *still in his TfL uniform, paces; he is distracted, pissed off.*

MARKOS. Which one is he?

FEVAN. Leave it Markos. It's done now.

MARKOS. It's the one with all the tattoos isn't it? He's the one?

FEVAN. I didn't get it. It's fine. Let's just move on.

MARKOS. They're idiots. They don't know what they're doing. They should be supporting / you.

FEVAN. It's done. Okay? (*Giving him her phone for him to film her.*) How do I look?

Beat.

MARKOS. You look beautiful. Ready?

FEVAN. Once you have lightly mashed it and simmered it down with the jalapeños, onions, garlic and the spices I talked about earlier, you're ready for the toppings! Again, a pinch of berbere, fresh diced tomatoes and bell peppers, crunchy red onions, and if you are making a non-vegan version, fresh yogurt and simple boiled eggs go beautifully with this ancient dish...

FEVAN *presents the beautifully constructed ful dish to the camera.*

(*Vulnerable.*) How was that?

MARKOS. Very good. Excellent. That was excellent.

FEVAN. I don't know. Let me see. Are you sure?

FEVAN *watches the video back.* MARKOS *tastes the food.*

MARKOS. Wow wow wow wow wow! Delicious!

FEVAN (*uploading the video*). Okay, I'm gonna upload this one...

MARKOS. People will love / it!

FEVAN. Yay! I'm getting some new followers already!

MARKOS. See? You don't need that pop-up.

FEVAN. Manny's right, you know, I'm so late with this. Since lockdown, people have started running entire businesses just on Instagram.

MARKOS. But what about your idea... the community kitchen table? Where the people can come together. What about that Fevan?

FEVAN. I wanna do something that's going to work without me having to ask for permission from people who don't know anything about food. I have to be a doer, / not a

MARKOS. You won't have to ask for anyone's permission, we can do / it!

FEVAN. Look, if all these influencers who can't even cook can get all these followers imagine how many I can get? I won't need no bricks and mortar.

MARKOS. No no no, Fevan, what are you talking about?

FEVAN. I can start doing supper club if I have enough followers. Look, people are already liking the video! This is what I need: straight to the customers without some bank telling me I don't qualify for this or / that.

MARKOS. But, our food is communal Fevan; it has to be shared with people, you know, together in the same space, from the same table and the same plate, not something on a screen!

Beat.

Fevan?

FEVAN. What?

MARKOS. Come, sit, sit, sit. I need to tell you something.

FEVAN. What's going on?

MARKOS. Nothing, / I

FEVAN. You're sweating. Are you okay?

MARKOS. No, it's just, I get a little… I wanted to speak to you about something /

FEVAN. What is it? What's wrong?

MARKOS. Nothing. Nothing's wrong.

FEVAN. What is it then?

MARKOS. I don't know how to say this /

FEVAN. Say what?

Beat.

MARKOS. I've been thinking, you know…

FEVAN (*almost to herself*). Okay…

MARKOS. No, yes, I have been thinking, and maybe I'm being foolish or just dreaming /

FEVAN. I can't tell you if you're being foolish if you ain't gonna tell me what it is.

MARKOS. Yes / I

FEVAN. You can be honest with / me

MARKOS. Maybe I am too old sometimes I / think

FEVAN. Come on Markos, spit it out!

MARKOS. Listen /

FEVAN. What?

Beat.

MARKOS. When you tell me your vision, your dream of making something, creating something for the people I really feel something in / here – (*Touching his chest.*)

FEVAN. Uh-huh…

MARKOS. No, it made me think you know – why don't we ever own anything here, in this country? We just live, eyes cast down from cheque to cheque, hand to mouth, day to day and never look up and see the sky and say I'm gonna be someone, I going to build something – and you make me think / that

FEVAN. I'm… glad /

MARKOS. Yes, you fill me up with / this

FEVAN. Yeah?

MARKOS. With the possibility of what we can do *here*.

FEVAN. I feel like there's somethin' else you're tryin' to say…

MARKOS. I don't want to burden you. I just want you to be honest with me

Beat.

I have some savings. It's not much, but it is something. You know, since I came here, I drive these buses in the day and the Ubers in the night and save and save, thinking I will go back home one day and buy the coffee farm where my parents were pickers. Even after the revolution, they were still there, picking and labouring. And I foolishly thought I could help change things there for people like them, but the truth is, only money can change things. Everything has a price, even life itself, so I leave my boy and cross the desert and the sea, thinking I will return home, buy that farm and give it to him, hoping he will one day own the land where his grandparents were farmhands, but that dream is gone now. It's gone. This war has turned us against each other and turned our country into hell.

Beat.

FEVAN. So, you were saving to return?

MARKOS. Yes, before this war started that was always my plan. I wanted to be with my boy. I didn't want him coming here through these back-alley routes. Those smugglers in Libya buy and sell our people like cattle. I saw it with my own eyes Fevan, young men being sold into slavery for as little as four hundred dollars. I tell him this but he didn't listen /

FEVAN. Let's get him a flight from Khartoum.

MARKOS. I don't think he's in Khartoum. That number he gave me, it doesn't work any more.

Beat.

FEVAN. When were you going to tell me?

MARKOS. What?

FEVAN. That you were saving to go back, when were you going to tell me?

MARKOS. You sound upset with me.

FEVAN. I'm not. But that's huge isn't it? That you were planning to go back.

Beat.

It's just a big deal you know, having a plan like that and / not…

MARKOS. I know, I should have told you, but the other day when I hear you speaking, I just thought… this is it… we can do this. Together. We can build something great. You and me. We can buy that shop that you want and make it into the restaurant like you said. I can do the electrics, plumbing, carpentry, anything you need. I am good with my hands. Your vision, your creativity and I support you. Together I think we can be very successful. What do you say?

FEVAN. A restaurant is the riskiest business, you know that?

MARKOS. Fevan, have you not been listening to me? Every day, people are risking their lives for the opportunities we have here.

FEVAN. Listen, most restaurants don't even last a / year

MARKOS. Ah, if this is too much, please forget everything I said. I don't want to pressure you.

FEVAN. You're not pressuring me. I just don't want you risking money you've saved for your son on something like this. That'd be / crazy.

MARKOS. We can make a lot more. I believe it in my heart. We could be business owners, you and me. If you do this Instagram thing it will only ever be a delivery service; your dream is so much bigger than that. And God willing, when my boy gets here, he will have somewhere to work, he takes after his mother in the kitchen, God rest her soul /

FEVAN. I don't know / Markos

MARKOS. Why do you want to do it on your own when we can do it together? I promise you, I will do whatever it takes. That shop you show me, you know it comes with that flat upstairs? It's perfect, Fevan...

Beat.

You and me... I think we can make it work. I really do.

Beat.

What do you say?

Scene Eight

A week later.

MANNY *and* ABDUL *are at an illegal warehouse party. They dance like they are in a music video and drink from a bottle of champagne.*

MANNY. Fifty!

ABDUL. C'mon / fam

MANNY. He thinks he's a hustler? He don't know nothing about / hustlin'

ABDUL. Tryin' to go on like he's still road. He ain't road! He's juss puttin' it on, thinkin' he's / bad

MANNY. Man was tryin' ta test us ya / know!

ABDUL *(spittin')*. He ain't a real one! I'm doin' it for the fam, he's doin' it for the 'Gram!

MANNY. Jheeeeeeeeeeeezzzzz! Man like Abz with the bars!

ABDUL. Nah, real talks though, that brea needs to know –
don't be chattin' greazy to mandem who are still on the road!

MANNY. Get me! Man said fifty like it was a big ting ya know!
Fam, if we want we can register the whole estate!

ABDUL. The whole of E3!

MANNY. Lightwork!

ABDUL. He's just let the wolves in the house!

MANNY. Did you hear him when we told him? Tryin' ta chat to me about shaky voice? *His* voice was trembling fam!

ABDUL. Tr-em-ba-ling! That's what happens innit; don't ever underestimate mandem!

MANNY. Ever!

ABDUL. Juss don't it!

MANNY. Fam, you shoulda seen Sneak's face when I rolled up to Red Flats in my suit; he was baffed! I juss rolled up in there, big-man tings innit; three racks in an envelope and dashed it at his head 'n' told him not to fuck with me / again!

ABDUL. Why you lyin' bruv? You didn't dash nothin' at his / head!

MANNY. Nah, real talks I counted it in front of him innit, 'n' juss dashed it in his car innit. He was still baffed.

ABDUL. How's that brea got all these yuts goin' country for him 'n' he's still drivin' that bruck-up Punto?

MANNY. Coz he's a dickhead / bruv

ABDUL. It's good you counted it in front of him bro, ca that brea would come at you again if he / could.

MANNY. Oooooh, see that?

ABDUL. What?

MANNY. That queen that juss came in?

ABDUL. What? Omar's sister?

MANNY. Is that Omar's sister?

ABDUL. Fam, don't you recognise her?

MANNY. Damn!

ABDUL. She's juss come back from uni innit.

Beat.

Yo, allow it. You're being bait.

MANNY. I'm juss buzzin' / still

ABDUL. I know. Can't believe we got all dem people on / it!

MANNY. Easiest seven grand ever, and the DigiCoin Tokens keep goin' / up

ABDUL. It's mad, it's nearly at three hundred dollars / already!

MANNY. If it carries on like this, sooner or later we'll touch a mill!

ABDUL. You're propa good at explainin' this ting ya know. I was like rah! Manny's on smoke!

MANNY. It was nothin' /

ABDUL. Bro, half the people on the estate wanna get on it now!

MANNY. It's not juss because we speeched them ya know; bare a them already been to the community centre listening to my man / innit

ABDUL. He didn't think about / that

MANNY. Did you hear him when he said 'probation' like a fuckin' Fed? / Dickhead!

ABDUL. He got finessed!

MANNY. Rinsed!

ABDUL. Boyed!

MANNY. Dealt with!

ABDUL. Bodied!

MANNY. Smoked!

ABDUL. He's not ready fam. Us man's gonna take over this / ting!

MANNY. DigiGold millionaires / fam!

ABDUL. Woi!

MANNY *looks across at the girl.*

MANNY. Yo, what was her name again?

ABDUL. Winnie. She juss finished uni – in where was it –
Glasgow or somewhere like that / fam.

MANNY. Winnie. Oh yeah, that was it. Rah she looks different /
boy.

ABDUL. What? You feelin' her, / yeah?

MANNY. Nah, she's juss been preeing man the whole time /
innit.

ABDUL. Preeing you?

MANNY. Ain't you clocked?

ABDUL. Nah fam, she smiled at me when she walked in / still.

MANNY. Nah, you're cappin' / bruv

ABDUL. She's movin' like she's on man

MANNY. She ain't on you fam. Why you gettin' gassed?

ABDUL. Nah, man's celibate anyways / innit

MANNY. Celibate?

ABDUL. Yeah, celibate / fam

MANNY. Since when?

ABDUL. I don't want no distractions / innit

MANNY. You're a weird guy / bro

ABDUL. Nah, fam, Keisha was always on to man, 'ah you're
always on your tradin' ting, dis 'n' dat, reh reh reh'. It was
long bruv. Propa distracting. I couldn't focus on my charts /
innit

MANNY. You flopped bruv. Keisha was / cool

ABDUL. Nah, bro, I deeped still. I juss need to secure The Bag
first and foremost / innit.

MANNY. You can do both / fam

ABDUL. Nah bruv, queens don't rate breddas who ain't got The Bag on lock.

MANNY. Thass bullshit /

ABDUL. It's real talks!

MANNY. Thass what breddas with no game say. Not all queens are about The / Bag.

ABDUL. This guy! You keep chattin' to me with them shifty eyes fam! Go chat to / her!

MANNY. I'm juss seein' wa'gwan

ABDUL. You're horse-eyein' / fam

MANNY. What?

ABDUL (*imitating* MANNY). This you. Propa horse-eyein'.

MANNY. Shut up / brevs

ABDUL. Go chat to her / bro

MANNY. In a bit / innit

ABDUL. You're shook?

MANNY. Nah, I'll chat to / her

ABDUL. We juss made all this dough fam. Hold your head up. What's wrong with / you?

MANNY. It's just, I'm juss a bit waved / innit

ABDUL. What, you're drunk? This guy! Propa / lightweight!

MANNY. I ain't gonna lie though – she's lookin' *sublime*!

ABDUL. I know. Come. You've got your wingman, bro. Let's go chat to / her.

MANNY. Nah, that's bait / fam

ABDUL. Oh shit?

MANNY. What?

ABDUL. See that? She's calling you over / bruv.

MANNY. What me, yeah?

ABDUL. Yeah, you! (*Shouting across to Winnie.*) Yo! Yeah. Cool. You / alright?

MANNY. Ah / fam!

ABDUL. Go!

MANNY. How do I look?

ABDUL. It's not about how you look fam, it's about how you carry yourself. You got this!

MANNY. I'm going over

ABDUL. Do / it

MANNY. I / will

ABDUL. Go on / then

MANNY. Cool.

Beat.

MANNY *goes over to speak to Winnie, cheered on by* ABDUL, *as the music intensifies and the party breaks out into a dance.* MANNY *finds his confidence as he walks through the crowded party, and* ABDUL *joins the dance.*

Scene Nine

MANNY *enters the flat. Tipsy and still buzzing as he watches the DigiGold X charts on his phone. He's made some more money. He is happy. He grabs some food out of the fridge. He wolfs it down as he watches a video of Hamza being interviewed about recent developments in DigiGolds X's ascent as a cryptocurrency exchange platform and his philanthropic work across Africa.*

MANNY *starts making the sofa bed in the living room. He is still engrossed in Hamza's interview. He pauses the video when he hears someone going into the bathroom. He hears the sounds of a man heavily urinating.* MANNY *is annoyed.*

Moments later, MARKOS *appears in the hallway and smiles at* MANNY.

MANNY (*almost to himself at seeing* MARKOS). For fuck sakes / man.

MARKOS. Ah, Emmanuel, eh men, it's late, / it

MANNY. What?

MARKOS. It's late / men

MANNY. What, you're tryin' to put man under curfew now, yeah?

MARKOS. It's not like / that

MANNY. Not like that?

MARKOS. Eh men, your mother – she worries about you when / you

MANNY. Yo, juss don't do that. I'm not a yut. Allow it with that kinda talk.

MARKOS. Ah, listen, son, / you know

MANNY. Son? You takin' the piss?

MARKOS. I'm not… it's just you remind me of my boy, Dawit. Ah, I miss him. God knows how I miss him. He had just turned fourteen the last time I held him in my arms; now he is a young man like you. It's strange, but I look at you and think of him. That's all.

Beat. MARKOS *turns to go, then stops.*

I can't sleep. He's in Libya now. He called me from there, and I just can't sleep.

MANNY. Can't you just get him a plane ticket or sumthin'?

MARKOS. It's too dangerous. If they catch him, they will put him into one of these mass prisons there. The trade in human beings is big business now. Big, big business. The Europeans pay them to run those prisons, and we Africans pay them to get us to Europe. The traffickers are drunk with all the money they're getting from both sides, and they've become evil. The conditions of those places… the way they treat people like us…

MANNY. Is he alright?

MARKOS. He's okay. He's a smart boy. I just need him to get out of there in one piece.

MANNY. I'm glad he's okay.

MARKOS (*going to exit*). Ah, I better let you sleep men. Just because I can't sleep, I shouldn't make you stay up, too, eh? Goodnight s–… Manny… goodnight, Manny.

MANNY. Goodnight.

MANNY *gets ready to sleep*. MARKOS *stops and turns back, wanting to speak again*.

MARKOS. Your mum tells me you are becoming successful with this cryptocurrency / things

MANNY. What?

MARKOS. This cryptocurrency / things

MANNY. What about it?

MARKOS. Your mother and I… are thinking of putting in an offer on that shop, you know, the one down the road; I thought maybe you want to get involved.

MANNY. Whoa whoa whoa. Wait. What? What do you mean 'we'? That's her thing, you know.

MARKOS. No, no, no, no. I just support her, that's all. Your mother already designed everything. Did she show you the plans she has been making on the computer, imagining what the place will look like?

MANNY. Honestly, I'll be able to support her soon. I'm not being rude, but you don't need to get involved, ya get me? That's her dream. She don't need no co-pilot.

MARKOS. No, it's okay, I'm here to help. Whatever she needs. That's all. Have you seen the designs for the place? Ah, it's amazing men – her vision. I'm Ubering all night and taking all the shifts TfL can give me, so I can help.

Beat.

So, it is going very well, eh?

MANNY. Yeah, look, man, you should probably send that money you're makin' back to your son or sumthin'. I told you, I can support my mum with the restaurant ting here. We're good.

MARKOS. You have found your way. / That's

MANNY. My way?

MARKOS. I mean your vocation. You are lucky. People like me get to this country, too late, and drift through this maze without how you say… a clue / of

MANNY. Yo, sorry man, it's just, I got an early / start…

MARKOS. Ah, sleep, sleep, sleep. You must be tired.

MARKOS *goes to leave, then stops.*

Just one more thing: I hear you help some of the people at church join this cryptocurrency things. They all say they are making money with it, and I am just thinking wow wow wow wow / wow

MANNY. What? You wanna join?

MARKOS. Ah, I don't know men, even my son tells me about these cryptocurrency things, apparently all the young people back home are all using it now, but me, I just don't trust these / things

MANNY. Trust?

MARKOS. Yeah, I don't know if I can trust this cryptocurrency things / men.

MANNY. How can you say you 'don't trust' something when you don't even know what it / is?

MARKOS. These things… it's like another language to me. / This

MANNY. What's stopping you from learning?

MARKOS. I don't know. / I

MANNY. That's why you're broke, innit.

MARKOS. Excuse / me?

MANNY. Coz you're ignorant, innit. Here's an opportunity for you to learn, but you think you're above / it.

MARKOS. I'm not broke. I thank God I have everything / I need

MANNY. Broke people say that shit to make themselves feel better. I get / it

MARKOS. Please, stop now, eh? In our culture, we don't speak to our elders like / this

MANNY. When was the last time you used actual paper / money?

MARKOS. I use it all the / time

MANNY. Yeah, *you* might, but most people don't. How do people pay for your Uber and your bus? They use card, don't they? What do you think that is? A kind of digital currency, yeah – crypto is no different.

Beat.

MARKOS. Well, everyone at the church, everyone around here on the estate, all of us, we are all proud of / you.

MANNY. Alright, cool.

MARKOS. Stay strong and keep fighting, and you / will

MANNY. Yo, I need to sleep, man. You finished, yeah?

Beat.

MARKOS *turns to exit but can't.* MANNY*'s words are too wounding for him to let it go this time.*

MARKOS. You are so hostile.

MANNY. Oh my dayz man, this / guy.

MARKOS. It's hard for me to try… you know… when you are always / hostile.

MANNY. Yo, I need to get to bed, bro. What do you want?

Beat.

MARKOS. That's okay, you sleep. I will not disturb you, but you need to stop this hostility. I'm not your enemy. I'm here for you if you need me. Me and you... maybe we need to start again, / eh?

MANNY. Need you? What do you mean 'need you'?

MARKOS. If you / need

MANNY. Nah, real talks: what do *you* have that need?

MARKOS. I'm just extending / a

MANNY. Yo, I ain't tryin' to be rude, but you're a bus driver, bro. I don't need nothin' from / you.

MARKOS. You think this is okay, to speak to me like this?

MANNY. You always come here all the time and take up all the air, man. I keep tellin' you I need to sleep, I got work in the mornin' 'n' you're still standin' there – what do you want?

MARKOS. I always thought it's because you are half. It's not your fault.

MANNY. What?!

MARKOS. You don't know anything about your mother's culture because you are half. / You

MANNY. Half? What? Is that the best you got? Move man, don't chat to me about my / mum!

MARKOS. No, you are still under her roof. So / you

MANNY. There we go. There it is. You don't think I see through all your bullshit? You want me to move out, don't / you?

MARKOS. Of course / not

MANNY. Don't lie, you want me to bounce so you can move out of your little basement room 'n' move all up in here, innit?

MARKOS. I care about your mother. She and I, / we

MANNY. Yeah, don't worry I'll be out your way / soon.

MARKOS. You're too young to be so angry.

MANNY. What?

MARKOS. That kind of anger will eat you up, son.

MANNY. Yo! Call me that one more time and watch what happens!

MARKOS. I'm sorry /

MANNY. Just because you bounced on your own son, don't mean you can come in here 'n' start draggin' it /

MARKOS. Please, let's / not

MANNY. Nah, you wanna come in here and play dad? Go be a dad to your own / son!

MARKOS. You don't know what you are talking / about.

MANNY. Yep, tell yourself that if it makes you feel better. Now, can you step out of the room? I need to sleep.

MARKOS. I came here so he can have a future. I came here for him. You know nothing about me or my son.

MANNY. Yeah, I know your son don't rate you. I know that much, at least.

MARKOS *is winded by this.*

MANNY *gets another notification. He checks his phone.*

MARKOS. No. You know nothing about me.

MANNY. Aight, cool /

MARKOS. You / don't.

MANNY. Whatever / man.

MARKOS. And my son, / he

MANNY. Ah bro /

MARKOS. No, I'm not your 'bro'. I'm your elder! You need to respect / me!

MANNY. Yo! Who you shoutin' / at?

MARKOS. You're just a sheltered little boy. You don't have the slightest idea of what you're talking about. You've never even been back home, to the land of your mother /

MANNY. Neither has she though. She grew up here with white foster parents, so don't try preachin' to me about my mum when you don't even know /

MARKOS. It's half of your blood but there is nothing about you that is like us.

MANNY. What?! Nah, you need to stop sayin' that shit, you're pissing me off now. Say that shit again and I'll knock you the fuck out. / Move!

MARKOS. You regurgitate this nonsense you learn from these videos on YouTube, and call *me* ignorant? You don't know anything about me because you've never been curious to ask, too wrapped up in yourself. You don't have a clue.

MARKOS lifts his T-shirt, revealing old scars and burn marks.

MANNY. Yo, what the fuck you doing / man?

MARKOS. Look. This is me. What I went through crossing the desert to get here and here, see, I was younger than you when I was shot, fighting for the country that I loved. What do you know about that? And then to lose the mother of my boy… What do you know about / losing?

MANNY. Nothin'. I ain't a loser like you / innit.

MARKOS. What's wrong with you? What happened to you to make you this hard-hearted?

Enter FEVAN.

FEVAN. What's going on?

MARKOS (*to* FEVAN). This is your son?

MANNY. Yo, what the fuck you chatting about bruv?

MARKOS. Call me 'bruv' one more time. Go on, call me 'bruv' one more time, / Emmanuel!

FEVAN. Markos, calm down. (*To* MANNY.) What did you do?

MANNY. What do you mean what did I do? Look at him, Mum! He's coming in here and acting like a / psycho!

MARKOS. Fevan, this is not how we raise young men in our / culture!

FEVAN (*to* MARKOS). Excuse me?!

MARKOS. Is this how you've raised him? (*In Amharic*.) *Baalagay! Ehhay / sidd!*

FEVAN. *Baalagay?* Markos, don't be throwing insults like that around; tell me what happened.

MANNY (*to* MARKOS). What the fuck you sayin'? (*To* FEVAN.) Mum, see? See what I / mean?

MARKOS. But, Fevan, is / this how

FEVAN. Are you questioning how I raise my son?

MANNY. G'wan Mumzie! She done raised a king bruv – what you chattin' / about?

FEVAN (*to* MANNY). Shut up you fool! (*To* MARKOS.) Focus on your own; God knows he needs you right / now!

MARKOS (*to* FEVAN). Every time I come here, he has *no* respect for / me!

MANNY. Then stop coming here / innit!

MARKOS (*to* FEVAN). Are you going to let him speak to me like this?

FEVAN (*to* MANNY). Manny, just stop! / (*To* MARKOS.) Markos!

MARKOS. He's trying to rip apart my whole life just because I drive a / bus?

FEVAN (*to* MANNY). Is that what you're / doing?

MANNY. He's lying, Mum!

MARKOS (*to* FEVAN). I open my heart to him / and

MANNY. Oh my dayz Mum! He won't let me sleep innit. All comin' in here 'n' chattin' / whass!

MARKOS. Chatting what? Chatting / what?

MANNY. No wonder why your boy Dawit don't wanna speak to you / bruv!

MARKOS. Whass? Whass? You were born here but can't even speak the language, and you call me / ignorant?

MANNY. Mum, I've been out there hustlin' all day long, yeah. I juss wanna / sleep!

MARKOS. And keep my son's name out of your mouth! Tell him. Fevan, tell / him!

FEVAN. Both of you, stop it! Just stop! (*To* MARKOS.) Look at you, you're shaking! You need to go in there and calm / down!

MARKOS. No Fevan, I'm always trying with him, always trying to build a bridge with him, but he keeps throwing it back in my face! What am I supposed to do? Tell me?

FEVAN (*to* MARKOS). Be the bigger man! You're here screaming with a child in the middle of the night?!

MANNY (*to* FEVAN). Oi, who you callin' a child? I'm a big man out here ya / know!

FEVAN. Manny, the least you can be is civil. Just be civil – why is that so hard for you / to do?

MANNY. You takin' his side now?

FEVAN. I'm not taking anyone's side. Fuck sake! I just want peace in my house!

MANNY. You always let these men come in here 'n' take over your life innit, Mum?

FEVAN. Excuse me?

MARKOS (*to* MANNY).You dare speak to your mother like this?

MANNY (*to* FEVAN). I'm telling you now, I ain't gonna pick up the pieces again this time.

FEVAN. How can you say that to me, Manny? I have *one* relationship, and you're trying to slut-shame / me?

MARKOS (*clapping his hands in disbelief*). Eh eh eh eh eh! (*In Amharic.*) *Balagay! Endeh! / Eheh sid bakeish!*

MANNY. Nah, Mum, you're lettin' *him* get involved in your restaurant ting as well now, yeah? / Him?

FEVAN (*to* MARKOS). You told him?

MARKOS (*to* FEVAN). Leave / him.

FEVAN. Markos! For God sake!

MARKOS (*to* FEVAN). He's drunk! I can smell it from / here!

MANNY. You're letting him juss come in here and start runnin' your / life?

FEVAN. He's my partner /

MANNY. See what I mean Mum, it's like you're… what was it… flippin'… self-sabotaging. How can you try going into business with *him*? Just like that? Do you think he has the slightest clue about business?

FEVAN. I'm not handing anything over to him. Why are you saying it like that? He's just helping me, that's all.

MANNY. Did he pressure you into this?

MARKOS (*clapping his hands in disbelief*). / Ehhhhh!

FEVAN. What do you mean did he pressure me into this? What do you think I am?

MARKOS. Eh? Twenty-one, sleeping on your mother's sofa because you lack the discipline or character to stand up on your own two feet, and you speak to her like / this?

FEVAN (*to* MARKOS). Shut up Markos! (*To* MANNY.) Why can't you ever be happy for me?

MANNY. I am happy for you, but I'm not just gonna say nothin' when you go and do something this stupid.

FEVAN. These days it's like I don't even recognise you / any more!

MANNY. What? You want me to lie to you when you're being bare reckless like / this?

MARKOS. If you won't respect me, you *will* respect your
mother!

MANNY. What, you tryin' to step to me? See this, Mum? He's
tryin' to step to me in my own yard! Dickhead!

MARKOS. Look, you've upset her! Apologise! Apologise to
her / now!

MANNY. See this? He puts on the nice-guy act, but underneath
it all, he's just violent innit. Go on show her your scars. Go
on. Look at him. Foamin' at the mouth 'n' shit! Don't let him
fool you / Mum!

FEVAN. Stop it! Both of you! Just / stop!

MANNY. Nah, fuck this. Get out my house bro!

FEVAN. Manny, just get to bed, we'll talk in the morning /

MANNY. Nah, Mum, this brea's tryin' to violate! (*To* MARKOS.)
Yo, you deaf? Get out my house bruv!

MARKOS. No.

MANNY. No?

MARKOS. No.

MANNY. Mum tell him. Tell him to get the fuck out *our*
home!

FEVAN. Manny don't.

MANNY. Tell him.

Beat.

Mum? Mum, are you gonna tell him?

Beat.

FEVAN. Manny, please don't do this.

MANNY. 'Don't do this'? You gonna let him step to me like
this? Tell him now or I leave.

FEVAN. Don't make me choose.

MANNY. What? Mum? It's *a choice* now? *This* is a choice to you?!

Beat.

Go on then, choose.

FEVAN. I keep telling you I have to have a life too, you know, Manny.

MANNY. Choose.

FEVAN. What? Are you trying to threaten me?

MANNY. So it's him? Is it him? You choosin' him, yeah? Cool. It's like that yeah? Okay. Fine.

MANNY *starts grabbing his clothes and putting on his shoes.*

FEVAN. Manny? /

MARKOS. Let him go! Let him go, Fevan! Maybe he'll learn something about life out there!

FEVAN. I'm sick of this, Markos! You can go as well! Both of you get out!!

Black.

ACT TWO

Scene One

DEVLIN *enters like a rock star to a track like 'WIN' by Jay Rock blasting in the auditorium and a spectacle of lights announcing his entrance.*

DEVLIN. Yo! East London's in the house! Wow! We out here! C'mon! We got people from my hood as well ya know! Leon! Yes, bredda! Roman Road, stand up! Where's my Malmesbury crew? Yeah, yeah! What?! Auntie Joan and Auntie Candice, you made it? Wow, everyone's here, boy! A-yo! I got my little boy in the audience as well; where you at Armani? Wave to Daddy – there he is, my little king, turned three yesterday – you can all wish him a happy birthday, and he's got a little sister on the way. I'm blessed. Truly. Me and my Queen Ny. Holdin' down the fort! Listen, I do these talks all over the world, and I'm tellin' you nothin' like being back home! So *grateful* to see you all! Welcome, welcome!

MARKOS *appears in the auditorium and sits among the audience.*

'Education is the passport to the future, for tomorrow belongs to those who prepare for it today.' That was Malcolm X.

What is crypto? Most of us have heard about it, right? Okay, cool, how many of you in this room *hold* any cryptocurrencies? Come on, don't be shy. Raise your hands. Okay…

I'm gonna be real with you. Crypto saved my life. I'm a kid from Malmesbury Estate who used to sell drugs all up and down these streets here and got my education locked up like Malcolm. I was in a young offenders institution. Feltham. I'm a statistical anomaly. I wasn't supposed to make it, but

I did, and I'm here to tell you that we're at the cusp of a financial revolution.

Big word. What do I mean when I say revolution? We've had the steam engine, electricity, the microchip, the internet, and now we have cryptocurrency. So, what is crypto? Simple, it's a digital currency. Your credit card, your bank card. What do you do with it? You buy and sell. But what makes crypto revolutionary? You can send and receive money to anyone, anywhere in the world, directly without no middleman. No banks, no Western Union, no nothing. All you need is a computer or a smartphone with an internet connection. Cool. How does crypto work? It works because of something called *blockchain technology*: the thing that's gonna change the world! Trust me, soon they will be using it to determine elections. Think of the crypto as the cash and the blockchain as the bank.

Wow. Quick pause. Sorry, I'm just having a moment. It's mad, innit? Me standing here talking to *my community* about revolution 'n' ting! This community raised me when the system gave up on me. And now I get the chance to give back to you.

This is why I'm here to tell you about our platform: DGX. We're the fastest-growing cryptocurrency exchange in the world. Don't take my word for it. These young generals will tell you. Owning a DGX Token, the native token of our platform, is like owning a share. When we grow, you grow. Community. Abdul, Emmanuel, when you lot joined our platform, how much was one DGX Token worth?

MANNY. Hundred and forty pounds /

DEVLIN. How much is it worth now?

ABDUL. Three hundred pounds.

DEVLIN. Three hundred. It's more than doubled in less than two months. Imagine the value in a year's time? In two years? Think of our platform like a digital Pardner. You lot know what a Pardner is?

What, we don't have no Jamaicans in the house? Rah, what's happened to the community? You lot know Auntie Joyce, innit? If you're from round here, then you know! She's tha original banker! You know what that Pawdna meant for us, Auntie? It was our safety net!

For those of you who don't know it's like a money club innit. Everyone puts money in, and then each member gets an opportunity to take out the full pot. It's not just a Jamaican ting. My West African brothers have Susu, and my East African sisters have Ekub. Different names for the same ting.

See, we've always had innovative financial systems in our community, but they don't want you to believe that. Our ancestors brought these innovations from the motherland as enslaved Africans to purchase their freedom. And we thrived with these same community-based financial innovations back in the forties, fifties 'n' sixties to buy houses and open businesses when the banks here used to refuse us loans. The same banks that made their money off slavery tried to keep us redlined and in poverty when we came here to build this country, and still, today, we face the same systemic barriers to financial opportunities. How many of you have tried securing loans to start a business or a mortgage to buy a home only to be denied and branded 'high risk'? I know I have. Bare times.

But what if I told you there's a world in which we don't need these banks any more? What?! I know, sounds crazy, right? Well, at DGX, this is how we are revolutionising finance.

Look to your left, look to your right, you can be investing in the person next to you, in your community, instead of giving your money to corporations and institutions who only see you as *a consumer*.

This is our community-based financial innovation for *today*. This is our *resistance*.

We can be our own bank. We can learn to trade and invest and have a chance at building generational wealth. That's the big picture.

But today, I'm here to tell you about something for right *now*. Today, we're launching a new feature on our platform dedicated to international money transfers: DGX Global.

Now, how many of you are using Western Union, MoneyGram, or one of them companies there? We been queueing up at the post office on Roman Road since I was a yut! You know these money-transfer companies are robbing us, don't you? We know that, but we continue queueing up to send money because there has never been an alternative for us. Sorry to swear, Auntie, but it pisses me off. This kind of systemic (sorry, Auntie) fuckery!

You're the breadwinner for family here *and* back home; you work hard and send money there, and they charge you five to ten per cent and call it a transfer fee? You send a grand to Yard, and you have to pay fifty quid jus fih sen ih? Ah wha? Fifty quid? That's a week's shopping! That's bill money! And then on top of that, your people dem haffi pay withdrawal fees of God know how much jus fe tek it out. You see what I mean? They're not getting that grand. They're getting less. Much, much less. See what I mean when I say systemic? Rules made up to keep people like us poor.

Abdul, your dad was sending money to support the family in Mogadishu, right? How much was he paying on transfer fees?

ABDUL. Somethin' mad like seven per cent!

DEVLIN. Fuckeries! Any of you who have tried sending money to anywhere in Africa know it's the most expensive place to send money to. Why?! Structural racism, that's why. No one cares enough about Africa to regulate these companies who think it's okay to overcharge you and me for sending money to support our families. But you know what? We're not having it any more; bun the system! Nah, let me hear you say that! I need to hear you lot say that because I know that's what you lot feel in your hearts! Bun the system! That's right! Bun the system! Say it again! Bun the system!

Yes! Today, we're launching DGX Global so that you can send money to anyone, anywhere in the world, within seconds, absolutely free. Your loved one can then withdraw the value in any currency completely free of charge. Not only that, you also get to check rates, track your transfer *and* even get back a fraction of the money you send.

This is a community-based platform where you're not just a user but also *a shareholder*. Imagine if all of us here in this room owned MoneyGram or Western Union, together with a global community of millions, and the more people join the community network, the more the value of your share increases. Building networks to build a financially inclusive future for *all*. That's what we're trying to do at DGX. It's not just a cryptocurrency exchange platform. It's a Pardner, Susu, Ekub for the twenty-first century!

Change starts like this. Us being in control of our own money. How do we at DGX benefit? Simple: with you, we get to grow our global network.

There is a QR code by your seat. Download our app, start using it now, and join our global community of millions! More than that, check out our educational packages if you want to empower yourself to *own a piece of the future*. I'm telling you, we won't get left behind again!

In the next five years, every tech giant, Google, Amazon and Meta, will try to launch their own cryptocurrencies, but we are the only ones thinking globally and holistically about how to make cryptocurrency and blockchain technology usable for *everyone*. Access. This is our innovation.

This is our revolution! Digital financial inclusion for all!

Scene Two

Later at the community centre, MANNY *and* ABDUL *clear up the space after Devlin's speech.*

ABDUL. Oi fam, did you tell her about this?

MANNY. Who?

ABDUL. What do you mean who bro? Keisha innit? She was all sittin' there screwin' me with her dad bruv. That brea don't like me ya / know

MANNY. Everyone from Roman Road was here, so / what?

ABDUL. He's one of dem breddas that voted Brexit innit. Dickhead.

MANNY. Fam, why you out here preein' gal anyway?

ABDUL. What you chattin' about 'preein' gal'? That's my ex / bruv!

MANNY. Nah, all you was doin' was tryin' to get some Snapchats! Don't think I didn't see you! How many people did you / register?

ABDUL. It's called networking / bruv!

MANNY. Nah, take that badge off bro, you're a sleazy / yut!

ABDUL. You're a pagan! Why you / hatin'?

MANNY. Bro, you know how many people I registered? Trust me, if them lot start usin' man's lookin' at a three-and-a-half K bonus minimum!

ABDUL. Is it?

MANNY. Mi-ni-mum!

ABDUL. Jheeeeeeeez! Is that you yeah?

MANNY. Bro, I got bare people from Mile End on it as well ya know! See Sneaks bruv? He was shook innit? Couldn't even look man in the eye! I registered his mum, bro! Rago!

ABDUL. Rah, you went in bowy!

MANNY. That brea is so dumb sittin' there with his mouth open. See him? This shit went over his head!

MARKOS *appears and sheepishly approaches them.*

ABDUL (*to* MANNY, *nodding towards* MARKOS). Yo…

MANNY *turns and sees* MARKOS. *There is a palpable tension between them.*

MANNY. What the fuck's this brea doin' here?

ABDUL. Chill / bro

MANNY. Nah, what's he doing here?!

MARKOS. Sorry…

MANNY. Yo, what do you want?

MARKOS. I wanted to talk to you.

MANNY. About what, bruv?

ABDUL (*to* MANNY). Chill, it's cool. You / alright?

MANNY (*to* MARKOS). Nah, you need to step off before I do you somethin' bruv! Tryin' to step / to me?

ABDUL (*to* MANNY). Fam, fam what's wrong with / you?

MARKOS. Please… your mother… she is so worried about you. Please… answer her calls.

MANNY. I'll chat to her when I'm ready. You need to get the fuck out my face bruv, I'm not in the / mood

ABDUL (*to* MANNY). Bro, man, chill it's / calm

MARKOS. It's breaking her heart. This silence. She wants to hear your voice. Call her.

MANNY *busies himself with clearing the space.*

Where are you staying?

ABDUL. He just got a sick yard in Canary Wharf uncle. You should see it. Your boy's / smashing it!

MARKOS. Wow wow wow wow wow Canary Wharf, eh? Praise God! Praise God / …

ABDUL. It's a little sublet ting until he gets that penthouse! (*To* MANNY.) Innit fam?

MANNY *ignores them, busying himself with clearing the space.*

MARKOS. Look at you both! Wow! How much you make, eh?

ABDUL. We're doing alright, uncle.

MARKOS. Praise God.

Beat.

Emmanuel, I just… I wanted to say… I'm sorry about what happened.

MANNY *ignores him and starts trading on his phone*.

ABDUL. Fam, uncs is sorry innit. It's bless.

MARKOS. The last thing I ever want to do is get between you. Call her. / Please.

MANNY (*snapping*). I said I'll call her didn't I?

ABDUL (*to* MANNY). Bruv, allow it, it's cool.

MARKOS (*to* MANNY). I would have… sooner, but they've got him. They've got Dawit in Libya.

ABDUL. Yo, I hear mad tings about Libya.

MARKOS. They keep asking for more money. I need to get him out.

ABDUL. These lot here have turned that country into one lawless place boy.

MARKOS. I send money, but it doesn't reach *him*. They just take it and ask for more /

MANNY. Is he alright, though?

MARKOS. I just need to get him out. He told me I could use this DGX thing and it will reach him.

ABDUL. I can show you how it works, uncle.

MARKOS. I just want to send the money to my boy.

ABDUL. You can do that, easy and you can invest in any cryptocurrencies on this as well, uncle, / look.

MARKOS. How can I talk with this Devlin?

ABDUL. He's busy. You can talk to us, uncle.

MARKOS. He describes these things very / well.

ABDUL. Nah, yeah, he inspires a lot of people still.

MARKOS. It's amazing. You know the world forgets us, but this DGX thing, / it

MANNY *makes some money on a trade*.

MANNY (*to himself*). Come / on!

MARKOS (*to* MANNY). You just made some money on this things / eh?

ABDUL (*taking out his phone*). DGX is very accessible, uncle; you wanna have a go? Lemme show / you.

MARKOS. You know I try to understand it, but it / still

ABDUL (*showing him the chart*). It's exactly like the money in your pocket, uncle, but digital.

MANNY. Obviously, he gets that, man; he's not that fresh.

ABDUL. Nah, I was explainin' it in the same way to my dad, innit. You'll pick it up, uncle. It's simple. You can learn all this on the DGX app. Start with the foundation package, and it will make / sense.

MARKOS. Ah, I don't know men. I just follow you.

MANNY. Hear that Abz? Man's on makin' that money, ya know!

ABDUL. Grrrrraaaaaaaahhhhh! Markos a hustler / ya know!

MARKOS. No, yes! Teach me. I'm serious.

ABDUL. Let's make this money yeah? / G'wan uncle!

MANNY. Man like / Markos!

ABDUL. Old-school hustler, yeah? Wanna see dem Lizzies?

MARKOS. Lizzies?

ABDUL. Dat gwap!

MARKOS. Huh?

ABDUL. Dat bread / innit!

MANNY. Money.

MARKOS. Ah yes, yes, yes the money!

ABDUL. The money, ya know! Man like uncs! You got this!

MARKOS. Yes! We do this!

MARKOS *gets a phone call on vibrate from* FEVAN.

It's your mother /

MANNY. You know my mum don't rate it. You better keep it on the low ca anyhow she finds out you're jumping on this crypto ting, you're done. Trust me.

MARKOS. I think I'll wait. It's better like that isn't it? Yes, that will be better. Please don't say anything to her /

ABDUL. C'mon uncle, we got / you!

MANNY. Say nothin' innit.

A flurry of handshakes, fist-bumps, and embrace between them.

Scene Three

Some months later.

FEVAN *and* MARKOS *are in an expensive restaurant drinking cocktails.* MARKOS *is dressed in a flashy outfit and appears more relaxed, confident, even full of swagger.* FEVAN *studies the menu with great interest.*

MARKOS. I always hear you talk about that famous / chef

FEVAN. I can't believe you got a / table!

MARKOS. Samuelsson the Ethiopian… I wanted to surprise / you

FEVAN. Look at this place!

MARKOS. Ah, I book as soon as I got Dawit out of that godless desert, but they make me wait months for a table here. These fancy places, / eh?

FEVAN. Look, he's called this dish 'Swediopian'; that's him, innit. Born in some hut in Ethiopia, then adopted by a Swedish family.

MARKOS. Swediopian! Yes! Order what you want. Whatever you / want.

FEVAN (*reading the menu*). Berbere-cured salmon, apple water, avocado! Wow! That's his life story on a plate! Look at this! He's called this one Addis / York!

MARKOS. Addis means 'new' in Amharic!

FEVAN. You don't think I know / that?!

MARKOS. 'New York'! He's very / clever!

FEVAN. Doro wot, ayib, fried chicken, and soft-boiled egg! My mind is blown – / literally.

MARKOS. Try it! Whatever you want. My treat! Do you want another cocktail?

FEVAN. I'm still working on this!

MARKOS. My boy's in Italy, we have to celebrate!

FEVAN (*still looking at the menu*). You know what, I might have to try a few things on here. Oooooohhhhhh, I'm curious.

Beat. MARKOS *takes out his phone and shows* FEVAN *the money in his DGX e-wallet.*

What is this? What am I looking at? What's going on?

MARKOS. I wanted to wait to tell / you

FEVAN. Is / that...?

MARKOS. We don't have to wait any more. I'm an investor in this cryptocurrency things now.

FEVAN. What do you mean you're an investor? Did Manny put you up to this?

MARKOS. No, I learn myself. This is probability. I'm good at these things /

FEVAN. How much have you put in there? /

MARKOS. Fevan, look, my portfolio. This one called Luna was a miracle, and this other big one I invested in, Solana, it gained over six thousand per cent in one year! Can you / believe it?

FEVAN. Markos, how much did you put in there?

MARKOS. Look how much I have / now!

FEVAN. Is this what you've been up to all those evenings you said / you were

MARKOS. Look! Look, one hundred / thousand!

FEVAN. Markos /

MARKOS. More than double what I had before, look, see?

FEVAN. Did you put all your savings on there?

MARKOS. This is good. Don't you / see?

FEVAN. Good? Markos, why didn't you tell me?

MARKOS. Look, this means we can make an offer on the shop. I already spoke to / them and

FEVAN. Whoa, whoa, wait. What?

MARKOS. What? What's wrong?

FEVAN. What do you mean what's wrong? You go and speak to them and don't even think to check with me first?

MARKOS. I wanted to surprise you. They said they'd accept three-seven-/five

FEVAN. You're making offers / now?!

MARKOS. I didn't make an offer. I just spoke to / them.

FEVAN. This is not us Markos.

MARKOS. What?

FEVAN. We talk.

MARKOS. But this is good news. No? Fevan? We put together what we have and we'll only need a small, small mortgage.

FEVAN. I told you. We should lease somewhere for a year and see how it / goes.

MARKOS. But we have to own something in this country, Fevan. That's real freedom. That place could be the beginning of how you say… generational wealth for us, for our / sons.

FEVAN. You're gambling /

MARKOS. It's not gambling, Fevan.

FEVAN. I've been with a gambler. I know what it is. I'm not gonna do that / again.

MARKOS. But, Fevan, you have to understand. This is the future of / money.

FEVAN. It's a pyramid scheme /

MARKOS. Look how much I've made for us.

FEVAN. Stop saying that, Markos. I didn't ask you to do that. To gamble away your savings like / that.

MARKOS. Dawit, when he was in Libya, this was the only way I could get money to / him.

FEVAN. Sending money is one thing, but you're putting your *savings* on there?

MARKOS. Fevan, look, I own a share of this whole thing. DGX. Do you know how big this company is? Fevan, I'm a trader now. I'm getting good.

FEVAN. You're already hooked, aren't you? You got that glazed look in your eyes. You're not even hearing anything I'm saying are / you?

MARKOS. Fevan, I promise you this is a big door opening / for us.

FEVAN. You know what I went through with Manny's / dad.

MARKOS. Why do you say that? You think I would steal from you like he did? Everything I have here is for / *us*.

FEVAN. He used to say the same things. Exact same things. That's what it does. It's the lies, the addiction. I'm not gonna do it again / Markos.

MARKOS. Lies? I would never lie to / you!

FEVAN. Is this why you've been so distant these past few months? You've probably been glued to your screen like Manny and Abdul. I can't believe you're on this as well!

MARKOS. How long are we going to wait and save? How long, Fevan?

FEVAN. Don't you get it? This is about trust.

MARKOS. Trust?

FEVAN. Yes, trust.

MARKOS. I didn't want us to miss out on / this

FEVAN. When we said we'd do this together. What did I ask you?

MARKOS. I know what you feel about these things / and

FEVAN. Not to keep anything from me Markos. To be open with me.

MARKOS. I wanted to make sure I actually made money before I show / you.

FEVAN. It's not just about money.

MARKOS. Fine. I'm sorry.

FEVAN. What are you sorry for? Are you even listening to / me?

MARKOS. I just wanted to make sure first because I know how you feel about these things. We have the money now; that's the main thing.

FEVAN. You think that's the main thing?

MARKOS. Fevan, we can't get left behind.

FEVAN. So, what happens when you lose that money? How are you gonna look your son in the eye?

MARKOS. How do you think I paid for him to cross the Mediterranean Sea? He in Italy now, safe because I can use this platform to send money directly to him. It's like I can hold his hand from here because of this. This is real, Fevan. Can't you see?

FEVAN. Markos, don't get carried away. Don't be reckless with something like this. Take your money off this platform.

MARKOS. But this is a chance for me, Fevan; why can't you understand that? I know it's a risk. I know, but I have to take that risk. Once we get a place here, we can buy the farm back home. We have the best crops. *Kassa Koffee*. We can build how you say, *a brand*, Fevan. Since I came to this country, what did I do? Stand in toilets selling chewing gum and perfume to drunks? They don't even look at me. I am invisible. When I become a driver, I think this is it. This is as far as I go, this is the ceiling for someone like me. I never thought I would see this kind of opportunity to own a piece of the future like they say. To be a part of it. To use my brain and make smart investments. To be able to afford to sit at this table. Fevan, this is our chance to be free. Don't you see that?

Beat.

FEVAN. Markos, look me in the eyes. You know what I've been through. Tell me I can trust you.

MARKOS (*reaching across and holding her hands*). Of course, you can trust me.

Beat.

FEVAN. Make the offer.

MARKOS. What?

FEVAN. Call them. Make the offer.

MARKOS. You sure?

FEVAN. Do it before I change my mind.

MARKOS *calls the estate agents.* FEVAN *nervously watches him. The wait feels excruciating. Then finally…*

MARKOS. Hello? Hi… James. This is Markos… yes… Markos Kassa, we spoke the other day. We want to make the offer. Three-seven-five. Yes. Okay. Thank you.

Beat.

(*To* FEVAN.) He said they will let us know by Monday.

FEVAN. Don't take any more chances. Take it out.

MARKOS. I'll take it out immediately. I have a good feeling. By the Grace of God / we'll

FEVAN. I need a drink.

MARKOS. I'll put it in my bank so it's not on this / any more.

FEVAN. Where's the / waiter?

MARKOS. No, look see? I'm taking it out. Withdrawing the funds. / Boom.

Scene Four

Some weeks later.

A small, sparse studio apartment in Canary Wharf. It feels cold and sterile. There is hardly any furniture. It feels like MANNY *has barely moved in, with only a few bags and clothes strewn around the space, a mattress with a sleeping bag, a rail with expensive clothes and boxes of new trainers along the wall.*

MANNY *appears stressed, glued to the charts on his laptop, while* ABDUL *puts up birthday decorations.*

ABDUL. Oi, you wanna go for a spin before your mum gets here?

MANNY. Bro, this article is / mad!

ABDUL. See it? Lamborghini Huracán Evo Spyder! *Grrrrrrrrrrrrraaaaaaaaahhhhh!*

MANNY. Do you reckon Hamza would do that?

ABDUL. What?

MANNY. Use everyone's money on the platform to fund risky trades 'n' that?

ABDUL. Come on man, what's wrong with you? That article's bullshit, bruv!

MANNY. How do you know it's bullshit? Look, Coinbase's sayin' they're liquidating their DGX tokens!

ABDUL. Fuck 'em. Haters innit. When the Binance deal comes through, DGX's going to the fuckin' moon! / Watch!

MANNY. Bro man, bare people been leavin' me mad messages! These voicemails bruv, / it's

ABDUL. Buy the dip, I got my dad to do the same. We doubled our DigiCoins!

MANNY. But this article / man!

ABDUL. Are you dumb? Haters bruv. Sayin' all that shit with no proof. It's politics /

MANNY. Yo, you need to stop chattin' to me like that. Always talkin' down to me 'n' shit. I'm not on it / bruv

ABDUL. I'm juss sayin' I been doin' this ting longer than you / bruv

MANNY. What ting longer than / me?

ABDUL. Buy the dip bruv; that's how you make money.

MANNY. It's fuckin' tankin', man! Look at this bruv! I'm getting wiped / out!

ABDUL. Bro, everyone's taken a hit. But it's gonna bounce / back.

MANNY. I don't know what to tell these uncles and aunties who put their savings on this /

ABDUL. Bare heads in the DGX chat are gassed! Inside info bro! HODL!

MANNY. I've all had to disable my voicemail. Bare fucked-up messages. Been tryin' to reach / Devlin

ABDUL. Look at Twitter. (*Showing him his phone.*) See this? Hamza's already tweeted. Look. He said: 'Competitor is trying to come after us with false rumours. DGX is fine. Assets are fine.' See? Don't be buggin' out like them freshies. The only thing you need to pay attention to is your wallet bruv, not some alt-right dickhead writing some bullshit / article.

MANNY. Nah, fam that brea was a legit crypto journalist /

ABDUL. Bro, this is *how* you touch a mill. Any cryptohead who's touched a mill will tell you: HODL. Hold On For Dear Life innit, but you have to have the balls to do / that.

MANNY. Nah, I hear that still /

ABDUL. C'mon! How you think Devlin got there?

MANNY (*furiously trading now*). You're right, bro; this could be a big opportunity. You're / right!

The intercom buzzes. ABDUL *goes to answer.*

ABDUL. Yo? Come up, Ms G! (*To* MANNY.) Check your wallet, bro.

MANNY. What?

ABDUL. All your DigiCoins are all there / yeah?

MANNY. Yeah, / obviously

ABDUL. See? It don't make sense innit, bruv? What that article was sayin'; if they're using customer assets for the hedge fund, why's your money still on there, untouched?

MANNY. Nah, you're right bruv, you're right, but we should have a ledger just in / case

There is a knock at the door. ABDUL *goes to answer it. Moments later, he enters with* FEVAN *and* MARKOS, *who carry a birthday cake and bags of food.*

FEVAN. Very nice son! Very nice. Wow, I'm impressed! Look at / you!

MARKOS. Wow wow wow wow wow! Look at this / men!

FEVAN. Look at that view! How are you affording this?

MARKOS. Em-man-u-el! Eh?

MANNY. I got a good deal. Sublet ting innit.

FEVAN. Where's all your furniture?

MANNY (*distracted by buying more DigiCoins*). Nah, I've ordered some /

ABDUL. I keep tellin' him, Ms G. Buy some art innit. Couple of frames here 'n' there. One of them sick leather armchairs here, man can look out and be like – yeah! The takeover! You feel me? You can be like, lookin' at all these flipping banks and be like Scarface! The world is yours / fam!

FEVAN. Where's your dining table?

ABDUL. Did you see my Lambo Ms / G.

MARKOS. Eh men, that is *your* Lamborghini outside? /Ah!

ABDUL. Yeah. You like it, uncle?

MARKOS. Wow, wow, wow, *that green* / Lamborghini?

FEVAN. Are you gonna take me for a spin then, Abdul?

MANNY. He got it in that bait colour, though? Lime green?

ABDUL. What you chattin' 'bout? That's the OG colour!

MARKOS. Eh men, let me drive it around / later

MANNY. After I have a go /

ABDUL. You don't even have a provisional / fam

MANNY. I can drive, bruv. I don't need one.

FEVAN. What, they juss approved you, juss like / that?

ABDUL. Nah, man's got sick credit ya know, / Ms G!

FEVAN. Abz in a Lambo / yeah?

ABDUL. C'mon! We're out here / Ms G!

FEVAN. I'm happy for you. For both of you. You've both done well!

ABDUL. My dad was shook when I drove it up to the estate. Man came out the yard like a spaceship had landed or somethin'. He couldn't believe it. And he sees me come out. Obviously, man's rockin' the suit with the shades 'n' ting, man's lookin' all Gucci 'n' that, and my dad was like – he was like – yeah bruv. Man was proud innit. Took him for a spin, and he's sitting there gettin' tearful. He had his own chop shop in Mogadishu back in the day. He knows everything about cars and that Lambo truss, drivin' it – he was gettin' all deep sayin' was like taming some wild horse. It was deep. Man was propa / happy.

FEVAN. He musta been so proud /Abz!

MARKOS (*accidentally pressing a controller and playing a UK Drill track*). This is your music, eh? See? I know, I listen!

ABDUL *dances to the Drill.* MARKOS *awkwardly joins him in the dance.*

ABDUL. Yooooooooo! Manny, you seein' this?! Man like Markos! What you tellin' me killa? This a sick tune, / ya know!

MANNY (*not wanting to dance*). Ah, allow me, man, nah, allow / me.

FEVAN. Turn that down. (*To* MANNY *and* ABDUL.) Are you boys / hungry?

ABDUL. Yeah, I'm / starvin'

MARKOS. Your mother's cooked up a / feast!

FEVAN (*to* MANNY). Where do you / eat?

MARKOS. We can sit on the floor, like back home. (*To* MANNY.) Hey men, I make samosa for you! Try it!

FEVAN. He was in the kitchen all day making these!

MANNY *gets some cushions for* FEVAN *and* MARKOS. FEVAN *lays out some food.* ABDUL *hungrily tucks in.*

Oh, Manny. Son. Your eyes!

MANNY. I'm fine, / Mum.

FEVAN. You're not sleeping, are / you?

MANNY. It's just been a bit / hectic

FEVAN. These people you've signed up, they've been turning up at my work, asking me about this DGX thing; I tell them I don't know, but they keep turning up. Greed, what it does to people, / it's

ABDUL. Yo! Some of them tried runnin' after the Lambo when I was takin' my dad for a spin. Them lot were movin' mad / bruv!

FEVAN. It's what this thing's done to them. Like rabid dogs, some of them.

MARKOS. No, Fevan, don't say that. They're good people. They all are.

FEVAN (*to* MANNY). You look exhausted. You need to look after yourself – both of you.

FEVAN *hugs* MANNY. *He melts into her arms like he is a child again.*

Are you settling in?

MANNY. People act weird when I get on the lift and / that.

FEVAN. They're just probably getting used to you /

MANNY. The concierge knows I live here but still acts like I'm some hood yut come to rob the place.

ABDUL. Yeah, fam, that brea's got an attitude problem; tried followin' man coming up here innit. And the mad ting is he's some African uncle!

FEVAN. He was nice to us, wasn't he, / Markos?

MANNY. Nah, dat brea is like Samuel L. in *Django*! He don't like / me.

FEVAN. Give him a chance.

MANNY. These lot juss ain't used to a young bredda living here / still.

FEVAN. Look how far you've come. Look at this. I'm so proud of you, you know that? Happy birthday / son.

ABDUL. Brrrraaaaaaap brrraaaaaap brrrrraaaaaaap! Grrrrrrrraaaaaaaaaaaaahhhhhh!

MARKOS. Yes, happy birthday! Elelelelelelelelelelelelee!!!

FEVAN. Come on, eat. There's plenty of food.

MANNY *goes to wash his hands.* MARKOS *follows him out.*

MARKOS (*privately to* MANNY). Is it true?

MANNY. What?

MARKOS (*quietly, yet with intense desperation*). This things they're saying about our money being used for risky trades? Is it true?

MANNY. It's not; it's just competitors spreading false rumours.
I wouldn't worry about it / man.

MARKOS (*showing* MANNY *his DGX account on his phone*).
No, but look, I've been trying to take my money out, and it's
still processing the request! I just want to take my money / out.

MANNY. Nah, it's only doing that because everyone is
panicking and trying to withdraw their money innit. The
system ain't built to process all these requests at the same
time. You get it? Your money is fine. Hamza's already
tweeted this morning all the assets are fine. Don't worry.

MARKOS (*visibly relieved*). Oh, my God, thank you. Listen
men, you have no idea – I was worried sick men. You sure,
yeah?

MARKOS *cheerfully joins* FEVAN *and* ABDUL. MANNY
*gets changed into an ostentatious Versace shirt before going
back in.*

FEVAN. Is he okay?

MARKOS. Yes, yes, he's / okay

ABDUL. You know what it is Ms G? Some hater writes an
article about DGX, and everyone starts buggin' out! People
are fickle, ya / know!

FEVAN. He looks so exhausted. Look after him, will you?

ABDUL. I will. I got a propa night planned for / him.

FEVAN. Good. Good. I'm glad. Just, no drinking – you're
driving now / so

ABDUL. Nah, man don't do dem haram tings dere Ms G.
Wallahi / innit.

MANNY *enters from the bathroom.*

MARKOS. Ah, birthday boy! Come, sit! Your mother has made
all this amazing food! (*In a posh voice.*) She is developing
her menu.

ABDUL (*eating*). Yo, I ain't gonna lie, this food is peng!

FEVAN. Thank you, Abz. You tried Markos' samosa?

MANNY *starts eating*.

MANNY (*eating*). Yeah, it's bangin'. (*To* MARKOS.) *You* made this?

MARKOS. Yeah, men. I used to make this for my brothers back home / men.

FEVAN. What, ain't you made enough to buy a / bed?

MANNY. I've juss been busy / innit

MANNY *gets a notification on his phone; he gets up and goes to a private corner to check it*.

ABDUL. That's sick.

FEVAN. What?

ABDUL. That view… that sunset…

ABDUL, FEVAN *and* MARKOS *look at the sunset*.

It's the same in my yard. Like a tower block sunset. Like the sky is on fire. That light is crazy.

FEVAN. Yeah…

MARKOS. It's like you can see to the edge of the world up here.

FEVAN. The light is always beautiful at this time of year.

ABDUL *gets a stream of notifications, and his whole demeanour darkens when he checks.* MANNY *comes back and eats quickly and hungrily*.

(*To* ABDUL.) Go on, have some more?

ABDUL (*now glued to his phone in a panic*). Nah, I'm good Ms / G.

MANNY (*to* ABDUL). Yo fam, don't worry, man! Trust me, bare cryptoheads are buying the dip!

MARKOS. The dip?

MANNY. All this panic is affecting the price of DigiCoin, so it's dipped, like gone down, you get it? That's how we're

gettin' to The Bag innit Abz? You buy that dip! I juss
invested in a likel Bitcoin, too; it's gone down something
mad, like over twenty per cent!

FEVAN. Bitchcoin, shitcoin, all these names! (*To* MANNY.) Oi,
you, try the kitfo.

MANNY. Yo Abz. Truss me, this is gonna be the year we'll
secure The Bag!

MARKOS. The Bag? Which / bag?

MANNY. Money innit.

FEVAN *puts food on his plate*.

Thanks, Mum.

FEVAN. Bitcoin and Ethereum /

MARKOS. Ah, yes, I understand, The / Bag.

FEVAN. I read that they are the only ones worth investing / in.

MANNY (*tasting the kitfo*). Yo, Mum, you have absolutely
smashed it with / this!

FEVAN. Really?

MANNY. Yeah! Mum, this is on some Michelin star level!

MARKOS. She calls it Afropean. Clever, / no?

FEVAN. Abz, are you alright?

ABDUL. Sorry, I just need to call my dad.

ABDUL *calls his dad, pacing anxiously*.

FEVAN. Does anyone want more food?

MANNY. I'm good, you know, Mum. Can I save some of this
for / later?

FEVAN. Of course you can. There's plenty for leftovers.
Markos, do you want a bit more?

MARKOS *doesn't respond. He is engrossed in his phone*.

Markos? /

MARKOS (*to* FEVAN). No, sorry, I'm okay.

FEVAN. Okay, everyone's ready for cake then?

A sporadic 'yes' from the men. FEVAN *goes to clear the food.* MANNY *gets up to help her.*

MANNY. Wait, Mum, let me give you a hand with that. (*As they exit to the kitchen.*) Yo, Mum, is it a chocolate / cake?

FEVAN. Yeah, I made your / favourite

ABDUL (*finally getting through to his dad, saying some words in Somali*). Yo Dad, Dad, listen, you have to log in to your account like I showed you. You remember how to log in, yeah? Yeah, okay, Dad, log in there and take out your money now… just do it now, Dad. I'll explain later. Just do it, Dad. Okay, alright. Bye, bye. Bye.

MARKOS (*quietly*). What's going on?

ABDUL. Everyone is saying to withdraw now. They're sayin' people high up at DGX are withdrawing their money.

MARKOS (*quietly*). That's what I'm trying to do, but look, it just says it's / processing.

ABDUL. It's doing the same on mine. We just have to keep checkin' for updates, but this ain't looking good, man.

MARKOS *and* ABDUL *are anxiously glued to their phones.* FEVAN *enters carrying an impressively crafted birthday cake, singing 'Happy Birthday'.* MANNY *bashfully follows her.* FEVAN *gestures for* MARKOS *and* ABDUL *to join in the song.* ABDUL *and* MARKOS *awkwardly join in.*

FEVAN. Are you going to blow out the candles then?

MANNY *blows out the candles.* FEVAN *cheers.* MARKOS *and* ABDUL *awkwardly cheer as well.*

Did you make a wish?

MANNY. Yes, Mum.

More notifications on MANNY*'s and* ABDUL*'s phones.* MARKOS *struggles to hide his panic.*

FEVAN. Go on, cut / it.

    MANNY *cuts the cake*.

    Wait, hold it there. Markos get in the picture. Abdul, you too, go on.

    ABDUL *and* MARKOS, *who are anxious and distracted, pose with* MANNY. FEVAN *takes pictures on her phone*.

    What's wrong with you two? Smile, come / on!

MARKOS (*to* FEVAN). Wait. You get in. Let me take one of all of you.

    FEVAN *hands him her phone, but* MARKOS *is already covertly checking his phone as he prepares to take pictures*.

    (*To* FEVAN.) It's okay, I can use this.

    ABDUL *sees this and wants to do the same*.

ABDUL (*to* MARKOS). Nah, you get in. I'll take it.

FEVAN. We need one with all of / us

ABDUL. Ready?

    ABDUL *takes a picture*.

FEVAN. Markos, you're sweating. What's wrong?

MARKOS. I'm / fine.

FEVAN. Abdul, come on. Get in. Group selfie!

    FEVAN *takes the group selfie and notices* MARKOS*'s increasingly darkening demeanour*.

    (*To* MARKOS.) Hey, what is it? What's going on?

MARKOS. It's fine. I'm just… I'm not feeling well.

ABDUL (*quietly to* MANNY). Bro, you checked your messages? They're sayin' for everyone to withdraw now, innit.

MARKOS (*quietly*). Who?

MANNY (*quietly*). Bruv, you just told me to buy the / dip!

ABDUL (*quietly*). Check the DGX group chat. It's fuckin' carnage right now, bruv.

FEVAN. What you lot whispering about?

MANNY. Nothing, / Mum.

    ABDUL *checks his phone and almost collapses from shock.*

ABDUL. Fuck!

MANNY. What?

ABDUL. They've suspended all withdrawals!

MARKOS (*in shock*). What? What does that / mean?

ABDUL. No one can take any money out. It's locked.

MARKOS. Locked?

ABDUL. Locked. Frozen. People are saying it's a rug / pull.

FEVAN. Guys! Can we all just put our phones away for five minutes?

    ABDUL *calls his dad but gets no answer.*

MANNY. No way. No fucking way. No way is this a rug pull.

    MARKOS *checks his phone.*

FEVAN. Markos?

MANNY. Bro, this is DGX. They would never do that with people's / money.

FEVAN. Come on. At least until we've had some / cake?

ABDUL. My dad bruv. My dad innit. He put his fuckin' pension into DGX! Anyhow this is a rug pull! Bro, I'm gonna go psycho!

MANNY. It's temporary bruv.

ABDUL (*trying to get through to his dad*). Fuck! Fuck! Fuck! If it is, bruv, if it is, I don't know what I'm gonna / do!

FEVAN. Abz, take a breath, yeah? We'll figure it / out.

MANNY. This guy! Bro, you were chattin' greaze about people buggin' out 'n' now look at you!

FEVAN. They've suspended withdrawals?

MANNY. Everyone fuckin' started buggin' out and crashed the whole fuckin' / exchange!

FEVAN (*to* MARKOS). See, what did I tell you? Can you imagine if you were still / using

MARKOS. No, / no it's

FEVAN. Users! /

MARKOS. What?

FEVAN. That is what these crypto companies call people, isn't it – 'users' because they know it turns people into addicts. Abz, breathe, it's okay.

ABDUL (*having a panic attack*). My dad, my dad, / my dad

MANNY (*to* ABDUL). Bruv, talk to me /

ABDUL. I need to go. I need to go find my dad.

MANNY. Bro, come on man, it's my birthday.

ABDUL. I got twenty-eight racks on this, and it's not even letting me log in / now.

MARKOS. You can't log / in?

MANNY. I got thirty bags in this, too, bro. Thirty racks / yeah!

MARKOS. The app… it's not working… it's not working. (*To* MANNY.) Look… / look!

FEVAN. Markos, what are you / doing?

ABDUL. This is why Coinbase pulled out. They musta seen the DGX / books.

MANNY (*voicenoting Devlin*). Yo D? D? Customer assets are always kept separate, innit? Let me know, bruv!

FEVAN. Markos?

ABDUL *calls his dad again, this time getting through to him. They have an intense conversation in Somali.* ABDUL*'s conversation with his dad continues throughout the scene until he exits.*

MARKOS (*falling apart*). It's not letting me log on. It's not letting / me

FEVAN. What?

MARKOS. The money. It's not working. It's not letting me log on to withdraw the money.

MANNY (*to* ABDUL). Bruv?

FEVAN. Markos? What / money?

MARKOS. I'm sorry, Fevan. I'm so / sorry.

MANNY. It could be one of these central banks pulled out 'n' fucked everything / up!

FEVAN. Markos, what are you sorry about?

MANNY. DGX is one of the biggest crypto exchanges in the world, bro. It ain't just gonna / disappear!

MARKOS. God forgive me. God forgive / me.

MANNY. Fam? Fam, we juss need to see what Devlin's sayin' / innit

ABDUL. I don't wanna hear none of his bullshit, bruv. I juss need my money / back!

MARKOS. I was meaning to take it / out.

FEVAN. No, you did take it out. That's how we got the mortgage. I saw the / statement.

ABDUL (*back on the phone*). Yo, Dad? Dad, can you hear me?

He goes back to continuing the conversation in Somali.

MARKOS. I put it back in. I just wanted to do it one more / time

ABDUL. Please don't… don't cry… we'll get it / back…

MARKOS. They were paying eight per cent interest. That's eight thousand pounds for the kitchen, and I wanted us to have some / contingency.

MANNY. Yo Abz, Abz?

FEVAN. Eight per cent interest… Markos, did you put all our money back in there?

MARKOS. I know this looks bad /

FEVAN. You promised you'd never keep anything from me.

ABDUL. Dad... wait... I'm coming now. Just wait for / me.

MANNY (*to* ABDUL). Yo, bruv? Bruv? Bruv, where you going?

ABDUL. Get off me!

ABDUL *rushes out.*

MARKOS. We just bought a shop Fevan. How are we supposed to turn it into a restaurant without / money?

FEVAN. Don't talk to me like I'm stupid!

MANNY. Yeah, watch your tone bruv.

FEVAN (*to* MANNY). You shut up! See what you've done? Do you / see?

MANNY. What do you mean, what I've done? I'm not the one going behind your back 'n' being stupid!

MARKOS. Eh? Are you calling me stupid?

MANNY. Yeah, I am.

FEVAN (*to* MARKOS). Were you just *using* me?

MARKOS. I'm sorry. I'm so sorry / Fevan.

FEVAN (*to* MARKOS). You held my hand, looked me in the eye and told me that I could *trust* you. Trust you? That you'd never lie to me. You said that.

MARKOS. I'm going to fix this. I promise I'm going to / fix this.

FEVAN. Your promises don't mean anything!

MANNY (*voicenoting Devlin*). Bro, bro please, I just need to get my money / out!

FEVAN (*to* MARKOS). You know what, Markos, you *are* stupid. You're so fucking / stupid!

MARKOS. It's my money, my savings. You still have your money. I put everything I have into *your* dream, don't call me stupid / Fevan

FEVAN. You are. And a liar too. What else have you been keeping from me?

MARKOS. You're not listening.

MANNY (*voicenoting Devlin*). I'm gonna lose my yard, bruv. They're gonna make me homeless! I swear down, you need to call me / back now!

FEVAN. I was doing fine, Markos. I told you I didn't need you. I could do this on my own, but you made me trust you.

MARKOS. You haven't lost anything. I'm the one who's lost.

FEVAN. I haven't lost anything? We can't get the shop now, you fucking idiot! That was our deposit you just lost! You took me took me for a ride. You've broken my fuckin' heart, and you're telling me I haven't lost anything? Are you for real?

MARKOS (*trying to make physical contact*). Fevan, please /

FEVAN. I don't even know who you are! Who are you, Markos? Who the fuck are you? Don't touch me!

MARKOS. It was for Dawit. It was for my boy.

FEVAN (*to* MANNY). What have you done? What have you done?!

MANNY. He was only meant to send money back. That / was it.

FEVAN (*to* MARKOS). I said don't / touch me!

MARKOS. It was for *us*.

FEVAN. No, don't make this about me.

MANNY (*voicenoting Devlin*). D man, please. Please call me back, yeah?

MARKOS. I told him not to trust this cryptocurrency things, but he called me ignorant! *Ignorant?* When I was trying to warn him, when I was trying to protect him!

FEVAN. Protect him? You can't even protect your own son!

MARKOS. Don't say that. Fevan, please don't say / that.

FEVAN (*to* MARKOS). I just feel so fucking sad right now.

MARKOS *reaches his hand to* FEVAN *to touch her.*

I feel like such / a

MARKOS. Fevan, please /

FEVAN. I can't even look at you right / now.

MARKOS. I'm sorry.

MANNY (*voicenoting Devlin*). Yo, / D...?

MARKOS. Please /

FEVAN. I *trusted* you /

MANNY. Mum? /

FEVAN (*to* MANNY). Don't. Don't you speak to me.

> FEVAN *rushes out.*

MARKOS. Fevan? Fevan! Fevan!

> MANNY *and* MARKOS *are alone in the space, surrounded by birthday paraphernalia and the uneaten cake and an unbearable silence.*

Scene Five

DEVLIN *makes his way to his car carrying a baby seat. Two hooded figures in balaclavas appear. They confront him. They take off their hoods and balaclavas; it is* MANNY *and* ABDUL.

MANNY. Oi! Where you going? Why you not answering?!

DEVLIN (*trying to get to his car*). Yo, what?! Who you rollin' up on?

ABDUL. You innit! What? What / bruv?

MANNY. I got people coming after my mum. You understand? My mum!

DEVLIN. Come out my face / man!

ABDUL. Swear down, I'm gonna go psycho! Where the fuck's our money / bruv!?

DEVLIN. Listen, I've already had the SFO, and the fuckin'
    police come to my yard!

MANNY. Did you tell them Hamza disappeared the minute this
    rug pull / happened?

DEVLIN. If I had known he was using customer deposits, do
    you think I would have just stayed / silent?

ABDUL. He's fuckin' disappeared off the internet with our
    money / bruv!

DEVLIN. The central bank wanted its money back. Hamza knew
    he didn't have the money, so he dipped into our pockets to pay
    them back. That's what happened. Some colonial shit.

ABDUL. Oh my dayz / bruv!

DEVLIN. Bankers crash the world economy and get bailed out,
    yet we have a little wobble, and they pull the rug from under
    our feet. This is systemic.

MANNY. What do you mean 'they'? This is *you,* bruv!

DEVLIN. It's not me /

ABDUL. That was supposed to be his pension! That was
    everything he had! / Everything!

DEVLIN. Nah, don't fuckin' put that on me! I've lost money /
    too.

MANNY. I don't care what you / lost!

DEVLIN. They don't want us to be independent.

ABDUL. I don't wanna hear your conspiracy theories.

DEVLIN. It ain't a conspiracy theory. Do your research. This
    technology is the biggest threat to them because they know it
    will democratise the global financial system and give power
    to the people. They know / that

ABDUL. Are you deaf?

DEVLIN. I need to go get my / son.

ABDUL. I'm tellin' you now, I'll put a brick through your
    fuckin' Rari if you don't tell us where you man put
    our / money!

DEVLIN. I told you.

MANNY. All that shit about oppressed people, but you used it against us, didn't you? You lot came after your own community bruv! People who had nothing to do with crypto lost everything because you made them believe in / you.

DEVLIN. Everything I've said I stand by. I can stand here and talk to you, walk through endz with my head up, because I know I've been one hundred with everyone. With *everyone*, ya / understand?

MANNY. You saw how desperate we were and you fuckin' butchered us!

ABDUL. Butchered us like pigs / bruv!

DEVLIN. Listen, the moment we try to rise up and do our own thing, they find new ways to put chains on us! Look at what they keep taking from us. Our gold, diamonds, oil, everything precious to them is *ours*, but what's not precious to them is *us*, our bodies and our lives. *That's what this is about*. But we can't give up. You understand? Another way is still possible, it's still possible.

Scene Six

MANNY *enters, taking off his balaclava and panting from the run.* FEVAN *is sat on her own.*

MANNY. Ain't you supposed to be working, / Mum?

FEVAN. You know I can't go to work. Why you asking me?

MANNY. Sorry Mum.

FEVAN. You've embarrassed me.

MANNY. I'll walk you.

FEVAN. With your face covered like a criminal?

MANNY. Nah, I'll juss walk with you innit.

FEVAN. I don't even know if I can go back now.

MANNY. Sorry.

FEVAN. Yeah, me too.

Beat.

I'm unbelievably disappointed.

Silence.

FEVAN *brings a plate of food and places it on the table in front of* MANNY.

MANNY (*showing her his notepad*). I went into the community centre. They said I could have the space on Saturday afternoon to speak to everyone.

FEVAN. The least you can do is be accountable.

Beat.

MANNY. Some people from the church tried to come up here earlier. / It

FEVAN. What? Were they in the / building?!

MANNY. Yeah, / they

FEVAN. How did they get / in?

MANNY. I donno but I just pretended I wasn't in. They stood out there for ages, all looking through the letter box and stuff.

FEVAN. What they gonna get coming up here?

MANNY. A lot of people in that church lost money / so

FEVAN. They're not the only / ones.

MANNY. Hamza's been / arrested

FEVAN. We all lost, didn't / we?

MANNY. It's all over the news, '"Crypto King" Arrested in the / Bahamas.' Devlin's sayin' people's money might be recovered / if

FEVAN. Someone in the building must have let them in. Coming up here like we have anything / worth

MANNY. It's not for you / Mum.

FEVAN. I know it's not. You made them dream... Those seminars... the story you sold... that's why they're so angry. It's not just what they've lost. It's because they have to return to reality... People would rather hold on to their delusions at any cost rather than face reality.

The intercom buzzes. They both freeze.

FEVAN *goes to answer it.*

MANNY. Mum, don't.

FEVAN. It's fine.

(*Answering the intercom.*) Who is it?

There is no answer.

Beat.

MANNY. I saw on Facebook some of them were trying to bring the pastor here.

FEVAN. They're still posting on / Facebook?

MANNY. Talkin' about 'We will hunt them down. And drag them out of their holes and make them answer!'

FEVAN. And they call themselves Christians?

The buzzer buzzes again.

We should go to the police with this. They / can't

MANNY (*going to check out the window*). I should just go out there and speak to / them.

FEVAN No. You don't set foot out of this flat, you hear me?

The buzzer buzzes again. This time more incessant and more aggressive. FEVAN and MANNY are both startled and fearful. MANNY cannot bring himself to go to the buzzer. FEVAN picks up the receiver of the intercom...

Hello?

A chorus of angry voices can be heard coming from the receiver.

It's them.

FEVAN *runs to check out the window.*

The incessant buzzing continues. We can hear buzzers going off in other flats. It feels like chaos is being unleashed.

MANNY. Mum, they're buzzing at everyone's / door

Voices can be heard downstairs. It sounds like a big crowd. MANNY*'s anxiety is escalating into a full-blown panic attack.*

I'm gonna speak to them. I'm gonna go downstairs and speak to / them

FEVAN. Manny!

We can hear footsteps rushing up the stairs.

MANNY. I think they are coming up the stairs!

Some moments later there is a knock at the door. The knocking continues. MANNY *and* FEVAN *are still; they do not dare answer.*

MARKOS. Fevan?

Beat.

Fevan it's me... I've spoken to them... they're leaving now... please don't worry... they know it is not his fault... tell Manny it is okay... I've spoken to them. They know... We just... we all thought we were getting into something that would help us. Give us, you know, the... financial freedom... but you were right all along, and I told them... I told them you were right... We all gambled, and we lost. I told them. You know they are all *good people*. I tell them... they have to move on... money isn't everything... they know that. These past few days I've been thinking about this passage from the Bible: *For the love of money is the root of all evil: which while some coveted after, they have erred from the faith and pierced themselves through with many sorrows.*

Ha! This is true, isn't it?

Beat.

This is what happened to us… The wretched of the earth.
I doubled what took me ten years to save. I had that in my
hands, Fevan, and I lost sight. I wish I could take it back.
I wish I listened to you. But I didn't.

Beat.

Fevan? Are you there?

FEVAN. I don't want to talk to you.

MARKOS. Ah, Fevan, ah, your voice. I'm so happy to hear
your voice.

FEVAN. I need time, Markos.

MARKOS. Okay, I understand. I… Fevan… Dawit is here. He
crossed the water and he's with me now. Can you believe it?
He crossed the desert and the sea in one piece. It's a miracle,
really. I thank God. I hope you'll meet him… he wants to
meet you too…

We hear the sounds of someone coming up the stairs.
MARKOS *makes them leave.*

I said wait downstairs! Go back!

(*Back to* FEVAN.) Don't worry, they've gone now. Fevan?
I can stay out here if you want. I don't mind. I can stay
outside and speak to them if any more people come.

FEVAN. You don't have to.

MARKOS. No. I want to. I want to be here, Fevan. I want to be
with you.

Epilogue

Some weeks later.

ABDUL *is outside on the estate, back in his old clothes. Canary Wharf and the financial buildings of the City are visible yet out of reach, like another country on another shore.* MANNY *enters with a kitchen apron on, running towards the flats and listening to a podcast on his earphones.*

MANNY. Yo!

ABDUL (*going in for an embrace*). Yo.

MANNY. Abz, man! You been off-grid boy! Off-road! Off the bits, / still!

ABDUL. Yo, I ain't gonna lie, you propa smell of injera / boy!

MANNY. Ah, bro, my mum's got me working at her pop-up on Roman Road. It's mad busy innit. I'm juss pickin' up some shit from the flat – you wanna come up? Get a juice?

ABDUL. Nah, you know what bro, I'm working innit. Forex / bruv.

MANNY. Man like Abz on the hustle yeah! I rate that!

ABDUL. I juss need to level-/up

MANNY. Forex trading, / yeah?

ABDUL. None of these lot are calling me back for interviews. Pagans innit. I'm juss tryin' to get my peas up fam. You get me; I need to pay my dad back and / 'n' that

MANNY. Rah, he asked you to pay him / back?

ABDUL. Of course not. C'mon man, what's wrong with you? I juss wanna make sure he's alright / innit

MANNY. Nah, I rate that / still

ABDUL. Whatever I make, I juss wanna give to him.

MANNY. That's real fam. You're keepin' it certi.

ABDUL. Yeah, big man tingz / innit

MANNY. How is he, though? He's alright, / yeah?

ABDUL. He's alright. Started working for Uber now, ya get me. He's hustlin' doing his / thing

MANNY. Nah, that's good / fam

ABDUL. That support group's been good for / him

MANNY. Yeah, Markos is all up in that all preachin' 'n' / shit

ABDUL. Dad said.

Beat.

MANNY. You gonna watch the / trial?

ABDUL. When is it?

MANNY. I donno bruv. They haven't given a date 'n' / that

ABDUL. If them man get convicted, they're lookin' at a hundred years or some / madness

MANNY. Defrauded bare people / innit

ABDUL. Defrauded people out of / billions

MANNY. Billions / fam

ABDUL. This crypto ting is fucked. Fulla wolves fam. Wolves looking for sheep.

MANNY. It's not crypto fam; it's *people* who are fucked.

ABDUL. Nah, I'm making peas off Forex now, / still

MANNY. What?

ABDUL. Foreign exchange trading innit. I'm gettin' / paid.

MANNY. You make a couple a bills 'n' you're Warren Buffett now / yeah?

ABDUL. You're a hater / bruv

MANNY. How much you make?

ABDUL. Nah, don't worry about that. All you need to know is I'm gettin' paid / innit.

MANNY. How much? /

ABDUL. I'm getting paid.

MANNY. Bro, I been listening to Tony Robbins. Bad-boy motivational speaker innit. He said: 'Most people fail in life because they major in minor things.' You get it? Minor tings; this hood shit mandem are on. You need to deep it fam. It's about buildin' your own ting. Your *own* ting fam. Us man shouldn't be on minor tingz any more. We need to think big.

Beat.

You know what?

ABDUL. What?

MANNY. I've been thinking innit.

ABDUL. Yeah?

MANNY. Hamza and them man didn't have the balls.

ABDUL. They did. They had the balls to fuck the world / bruv.

MANNY. Nah, they didn't. They bottled it, bruv. They could have changed the world, bro. They could have empowered everyday people and helped the community level-up, but they bottled it.

ABDUL. It was all bullshit / anyway

MANNY. It weren't fam. You ever seen that many breddas all inspired, all in one space, all looking to change the world like that? He had that, and he / bottled it.

ABDUL. What you chattin' about? It was some flippin' multi-level marketing scam with a fairytale thrown in; no one was gonna change shit.

MANNY. Nah, it was real.

Beat.

The vision was real.

Beat.

I'm gonna start my own ting innit. Do what Hamza and them man didn't have the balls to do. I'm gonna build something that works for everyone from here in endz to all the way for people in Africa, bruv. Bitcoin's back up innit, did you see? Sixty-four racks! What does that tell you? This shit is here to stay.

ABDUL. Ah, bro, man, allow / me.

MANNY. Nah, all the madness we've been through propa opened my eyes innit. Governments 'n' banks everywhere been controlling and manipulating money and fucking with people for time. But, deep it, something like Bitcoin bro, it legit takes the power away from the few and gives it to the many. That's change. Think about it; we have the blueprint, and we can create a platform that can help everyone be a part of it and benefit from / it.

ABDUL. Nah, thass a hype / bro.

MANNY. Everything that DGX was supposed to be, bro, we can / do.

ABDUL. 'We'? Rah, fam, I can't believe you're still on this crypto / shit?

MANNY. Nah, think about it, bro: why do they get to keep us broke 'n' use our money to fund wars 'n' shit?? Yo, if we control our money, we control our future. You get it?

ABDUL. Nah, don't bring me into it bruv. You're lucky Sneak's mum didn't get what the ting was about. Can you imagine if she put money in? You forget, don't / you?

MANNY. What, you wanna be stuck here 'n' be some bummy guy like Sneaks for the rest of your / life?

ABDUL. Shut up /

MANNY (*taking* ABDUL's *phone*). Hit thirty-five 'n' still be trading Forex on your phone 'n' / shit

ABDUL. Yo!

MANNY. Still couchin' on the block while man like me will be out there changing the world / fam?

ABDUL. Bro, swear down, don't make me grips you / ya know!

MANNY (*playfully*). What, you start goin' gym and think you're / bad?

ABDUL. I've been doin' jiu-jitsu fam, don't watch that, I'll grips you up ya / know.

MANNY. Jiu-jitsu? What, bare man sittin' on your face? I'll box you in your head / bruv!

ABDUL. You're a pagan / fam!

ABDUL and MANNY playfully grapple. ABDUL has the better of MANNY.

MANNY. Yo Abz! Abz!

ABDUL. Tap out!

MANNY. What?

ABDUL. Tap out!

MANNY. Me tap out? You mad, bruv? Never!

They continue to playfight like cubs in the wild as the lights fade.

End.

A Nick Hern Book

Wolves on Road first published in Great Britain in 2024 as a paperback original by Nick Hern Books Limited, The Glasshouse, 49a Goldhawk Road, London W12 8QP, in association with the Bush Theatre, London, and Tamasha

Cover photograph by Courtney Phillip

Designed and typeset by Nick Hern Books, London
Printed in Great Britain by Mimeo Ltd, Huntingdon, Cambridgeshire PE29 6XX

A CIP catalogue record for this book is available from the British Library

ISBN 978 1 83904 413 7

Woodland
CARBON
www.woodlandcarbon.co.uk
NICK HERN BOOKS
Printed on Carbon Captured paper

www.nickhernbooks.co.uk/environmental-policy

www.nickhernbooks.co.uk

@nickhernbooks